Revenue Growth

*A Management Guide For
Government Contractors*

Gary A Dunbar

iUniverse, Inc.
Bloomington

REVENUE GROWTH

A MANAGEMENT GUIDE FOR GOVERNMENT CONTRACTORS

iUniverse books may be ordered through booksellers or by contacting:

iUniverse
1663 Liberty Drive
Bloomington, IN 47403
www.iuniverse.com
1-800-Authors (1-800-288-4677)

Because of the dynamic nature of the Internet, any web addresses or links contained in this book may have changed since publication and may no longer be valid. The views expressed in this work are solely those of the author and do not necessarily reflect the views of the publisher, and the publisher hereby disclaims any responsibility for them.

Any people depicted in stock imagery provided by Thinkstock are models, and such images are being used for illustrative purposes only.

Certain stock imagery © Thinkstock.

ISBN: 978-1-4759-6919-1 (sc)
ISBN: 978-1-4759-6920-7 (e)

Printed in the United States of America

iUniverse rev. date: 2/21/2013

READ THIS BOOK IF YOU:

- Already win U.S. government contracts.

- Want to improve business operations on Small Business, Set Aside contracts

- Create, manage, and submit proposals for government contracts.

- Position your firm to win contracts.

- Develop your company's strategy to that end.

- Think about getting into government contracting.

- Think about getting out of government contracting.

- Expect to work on a government-funded project and have little or no background in that field.

- Work now on one or more government projects -- and want to build on that success.

- Work in a firm that does both commercial and government business.

- Work in a firm that does only government business.

- Deliver the technical scope of work on a government contract.

- Are responsible for project management on a government contract.

- Are responsible for financial and budget management on one or more government contracts.

- Work for the government with contractors or want to know more about how contractors run their businesses.

- Want to get better at winning and performing on federal contracts.

- Know nothing about federal contracting, but are intrigued by the possibilities.

Acknowledgements

Paul Serotkin, co-owner and EVP for an Inc. 500 (#141) government contractor, was surprisingly encouraging after being the first person to read the very first draft and his positive reaction and continued interest is one of the most important reasons that this work has been completed.

Jim Tierney, my co-founding partner in ClientView has provided support, encouragement, ideas and significant contributions to content, organization and structure of this work for which I am very grateful.

Ed Harrington, also a ClientView partner but more importantly a retired Army Brigadier General with more than 30 years of experience in government acquisition, procurement, and contract management provided detailed reviews and most important assured me that the content of this work is needed in the community of government contractors.

Joseph Lawler was the first CEO that I worked for and, while I did not recognize it at the time, was also the best CEO I ever met. He taught by example and it was his leadership that launched my life-long learning about revenue growth.

Bill Freeman was my direct supervisor for several years and from him I learned that a span of control over 600 people at a level of full and total understanding of the most minute details is quite possible and that it also was a capability I would never master. But he also taught by his own example that how to identify one's own weaknesses and effectively delegate to others.

David Griffiths performed a miracle of transforming this work from a difficult tome into a readable book. It is his copy editing skills and knowledge that are responsible for the readability of this book.

Claire Dunbar is only my partner, supporter, trusted advisor, critic, soul-mate and wife without whom this small book would still be just scraps on my desk.

CONTENTS

PREFACE

This book explains how firms who contract with the United States government can achieve consistent, long-term revenue growth. It is written for:

- Government contractors, their employees, and their leaders.
- More than 600,000 firms registered in the FCR which has recently been subsumed into the System for Award Management, www.sma.gov.[1]
- Firms in the more than 7,000 audits of Government contractors by DCAA during 2011.[2]
- The 1,715 firms listed in the 2012 August issue of the NDIA 2012 MEGA DIRECTORY.[3]
- All the other entities supporting the departments, agencies, and offices that serve the United States Government.

This is the first in a planned series of books addressing the practical issues of growing a business involving government contracting. Future volumes will be:

- Marketing for government contractors
- Positioning for government contractors
- Proposing for government contractors

Allow me to disclose where this primer fits in the broad category of business books. While researching it, I visited the business section of two retail bookstores: The Harvard Coop in Harvard Square in Cambridge, Mass., and the Barnes & Noble bookstore at the Palisades Mall in Nyack, N.Y. At the Coop I found about 7,000 business books arranged in 11 categories, and at Barnes & Noble nearly 2,000 in seven categories.

All addressed business in a generic or general sense. That is, not one was solely about a specific type of business. To be sure, that's just an observation, not a criticism, as most appeared to provide legitimately useful information. But there were no titles such as "How to Operate and Manage an Automobile Repair Garage," or "Management of a Lobster Pound," or "Revenue Growth for Government Contracting Firms."

I just want you to appreciate that my effort isn't in the dominant

FCR - Federal Contractor Registry (Previously CCR)

DCAA - Defense Contract Audit Agency

NDIA - National Defense Industrial Association

This book may be used as a textbook for a training program.

This book may be used as a reference manual that is a source of information on specific topics of interest to you.

This book may not be used as a novel to be read from cover to cover as there is no particular plot or surprise ending.

This book may not be used as a detailed guide through the maze of Federal Acquisition Regulations

This book does not explain all of the 16 procurement scenarios used by the United States Government; instead, it focuses on Full and Open Competitive Procurements. The reason for this is simple, that is where the money is.

current of business books, but rather in a large eddy. If your interests lie there, then this is the book for you. I know of no other such book aimed at the burgeoning audience of buyers and sellers in the government contracting game.

Another conditional note that must be mentioned is the United States economy at the time of this book's first printing. Without advocating any political leaning, I believe there will be a reduction in the Government's spending and a significant change in the almost unbroken patterern of annual spending and debt increases. However, even with these issues to be resolved, the United States will remain a very significant customer for the sellers of goods and services. The content and examples that are presented here will remain valid and useful as these problems are solved and into the future beyond.

Finally, let me introduce myself. I am Gary A. Dunbar,[4] a partner in ClientView LLC. We are a consulting company that helps government contractors align their business practices and culture with their major clients, and follow disciplined business development practices. This book is based on my experience as a CEO, COO, and general manager at various government contracting firms, as well as the work of ClientView LLC consultants. Please visit www.clientviewconsulting.com for more information about the firm and its partners.

INTRODUCTION

The eight chapters in this book are aimed at helping business leaders understand -- and profit from -- government contracting. The examples I call on are just that -- examples. Please do not take them as a straitjacket, no-deviations-allowed formula for running a government contracting firm. Indeed, each contractor is different and must fashion its own path to success. The examples in these chapters show one way to resolve the key management issues, with the intent that readers apply lessons learned as they see fit in their own unique circumstances.

Chapter One presents a model for consistent, long-term revenue growth, and it's been exceeded many times by many of ClientView's clients and almost all of the current slate of large government contractors. Chapter Two delves into a firm's revenue growth leadership and culture and the use of such tools as recognition and incentives to motivate higher performance.

Leaders and employees in almost every firm have varied backgrounds, and that can hamper business development. So Chapter Three looks into the need for a common vocabulary and effective teamwork. And since revenue growth is impossible without competitive pricing, Chapter Four explores the financial side of government contracting.

Chapter Five explains that some firms are successful because they consistently view the costs of business development as investments aimed at a handsome return. Chapter Six presents an overview and URLs for various sources of acquisition and procurement information as well as a summary review of the government's sixteen Acquistion Process Scenarios. Chapter Seven summarizes the steps to get into government contracting, and Chapter Eight has endnotes.

Major chapters close with a short self-assessment to review the material and get readers thinking about how the ideas apply to their own firms.

This book is built around a hypothetical -- but relevant in its details -- company. Using an actual company would risk offending the owners, managers, and employees. Therefore, FIRM is a fictitious company

Key Topics
- Chapter Overview
- FIRM
- Your Business and this Book
- Self Assessment Review

FIRM

not incorporated in any state or government jurisdiction. Nor is anything similar to FIRM on Google, Yahoo, or Bing. Rather, it's a composite of many firms that ClientView and it's partners have had the pleasure of working for or consulting with during our careers.

FIRM operates under the direction of its three founders and owners:

- Stratford Tegy, president and CEO, often referred to as Strategy
- Opie Ratons, COO, often referred to as Operations
- Marten Muniman, CFO, often referred to as Money

FIRM owes its genesis to events and episodes that have actually happened in my own career. In the real world that our readers inhabit, revenue growth strategies will, of course, differ for firms in different situations.

A crucial point to keep in mind: This book is all about the reality of boosting revenue in the government market -- NOT hypothetical or theoretical revenue growth. In that spirit, consider the growth strategies for a large organization with a win rate for competitive government procurements of 90 percent compared to a medium-size firm with a win rate of 20 percent. Or consider a start-up, wholly owned subsidiary with no contracts compared to an established small business with declining revenue. Without any more details, we can safely assume that the strategies of each firm will vary significantly. The point is that each firm will have a different history, financial status, set of capabilities, market position and ambitions. Our objective is to provide information and examples that may help each firm devise its own unique strategy and approach.

Your business and this book

For a management team striving to build company value, two key factors are revenue growth and return on investment from business development expenditures. Are your business development efforts being translated into increased company value? Below is a shorthand way to score the relationship between revenue growth, business development return on investment (ROI), and company value.

Revenue Growth

What is the average annual rate of revenue growth over the past four years for your firm or profit center division?

Figure 1.1 What is your firm's level of revenue growth?

Growth Rate	Score
0 percent or less	- 10
0 to 5 percent	-5
5 to 10 percent	0
10 to 15 percent	4
10 to 20 percent	7
20 percent or above	10

As you can see, a decline in revenue has an obvious impact, and even the second category of zero or minimal growth is actually just barely staying ahead of inflation.

Consider, of course, that revenue growth varies from year to year for most firms, which may mean that one year's figure matches or is less than inflation. Look at your firm's specific performance and adjust the scoring numbers as appropriate. You may also need to adjust the scoring for the last three categories of growth scores of 4 through 10 if your year-to-year numbers vary significantly.

Next, what is your average win rate for competitive contracts? Measure your win rate using the maximum potential revenue of all submitted proposals in a given time period compared to the proposals you win. (WARNING: If your firm does not rigorously track win rate, you need to take a close look at improving your business development scheme.) Also note that repeat business, while extremely important, is not likely to be a good indicator of increasing equity value since often it is simply replacing revenue that is lost when the contract period of performance ends.

Figure 1.2 What is your firm's contract win rate level?

Win Rate	Score
0 to 10 percent	-5
10 to 25 percent	0
25 to 38 percent	4
38 to 50 percent	7
50 to 65 percent	10
65 percent and higher	7

You can measure win rate by using a rolling two-year period and measuring both number of proposals won divided by number of proposals submitted, and by total maximum contract value (all options and potential modifications) won divided by total contract value submitted. Both methods yield different results and are necessary to obtain a clear measurement of business development performance.

But, you may ask, why does the score drop back down for the 65 percent performance and higher? Think about it: If you're winning more than 65 percent of competitive proposals, it may be time to expand your position in the market by increasing the number of contracts you compete for and/or diversifying your revenue base.

Or maybe you're just being too conservative -- proposing only on the safest opportunities. In other words, your firm or profit center division is failing to achieve the full potential of revenue growth.

-15 to 0 -- Your revenue growth and business development performance are degrading your firm's value. You should consider

5

postponing any sale or merger activities and determine how -- and if -- you can get more revenue. Do something quickly and thoroughly to overhaul your business development approach.

1 to 10 -- Revenue growth and new contracts performance are unlikely to be major factors in gauging the value of your firm. Instead, unique intellectual property or patents may be the best way to set that value. If you don't have unique assets you should delay sale or merger for two or three years until you can establish the ability to grow revenue.

11 to 17 -- Revenue growth and new contracts will be positive valuation factors. Still, you might consider delaying sale or merger for 18 months while you work on boosting business development performance.

18 to 20 -- Shop for the yacht! You've developed enough new business and brought in enough revenue to command a premium value for your firm. Taking corrective action is no longer on your agenda. But still, stick with your method of business development and look for ways to improve even more.

Buying things

Doing business with the federal government may appear to be an endless maze of forms, procedures, regulations, and opaque processes. But -- and this may surprise you -- if we step back and look at ourselves, we find that much of what the government does mirrors what we do as individuals when we buy things.

Take me as an example. Once I earned my degree (Master of Architecture, MIT '66), what I most wanted to buy with my first paycheck was a new pair of shoes. Sounds rather mundane, doesn't it? Not for me. The entire final semester, I had hand-cut scraps of cardboard every week and shoved them into my soles to protect my feet from exposure as the holes got bigger and bigger.

But the choice was hardly straightforward. Shoes come in seemingly infinite variety: types (sandals, sneakers, casual, dress, tuxedo), colors (even in various shades of brown or black for men), and quality ranging from high to shoddy. And of course, prices: How much could I afford to pay out of that first somewhat measly paycheck?

Black wing tips with thick leather soles met all my requirements. The soles would wear for a long time and I could always replace them when they wore thin (unlike most of today's shoes, I could put new half-soles on them). The style and color smacked of adulthood and career – no more student sneakers or loafers. And I could buy them at a reduced price in Filene's basement.

The way I made that long-ago purchase isn't that far removed from the way the government buys, given that the former was more informal than the latter:

- NEED -- The government demands that NEED be well-documented, reviewed in detail, and approved before it launches the procurement process.

- ALTERNATIVES -- Only after NEED is resolved does the government identify, analyze, document, review, and approve ALTERNATIVES, which always include defining the product and/or service to address the NEED. Just as important is the method chosen to obtain the products and services -- see the 16 acquisition scenarios in Chapter Six. The government also surveys the market to find out if it can even count on adequate providers.

- SOLUTION -- Only after the first two steps are taken does the government approve the SOLUTION. That is the act of obtaining the products and services at a price the government believes is reasonable and realistic -- at an acceptable level of risk.

Of course, as an individual shopper, you understand that the cheapest car available may not last as long as you want, or be as safe as you would like. But you also know that the highest-priced car may offer features that are not worth the added costs. Think like that, and you're doing exactly what the government does, but with much less paperwork. For its part, the government's paperwork helps ensure that taxpayers' money is spent wisely, efficiently, and legally.

- Is your firm tracking and accurately measuring revenue growth rate and new contract win rate?
- If not, is your firm doing something similar that serves the same function?
- If "no" to both, would those performance metrics help your firm
- What are the three most significant benefits your firm would get by adopting the two metrics?
- What are the three biggest obstacles to doing so?
- Who, in your firm, would be likely to support using both performance metrics?
- Who would resist them?
- What are the three most important things that must happen for your firm to use the metrics for three consecutive years or longer?

Self Assessment Review

CONSISTENT LONG-TERM REVENUE GROWTH

Stratford Tegy, the visionary who led the startup of FIRM (see Introduction for background), had heard about government contractors who grew firms at rates of 20 percent to 40 percent year over year. So he looked into the stories of the five actual firms described below (firms that benefited from the leadership and consultation of ClientView's partners), and created a model to launch and develop FIRM. Several examples in which ClientView partners have been key participants include:

- An established engineering firm with commercial, state, and municipal clients over a wide area won its first federal government contract, a three-year deal with a maximum value of $13 million -- thanks to a new environmental program created by Congress. The firm fulfilled the contract to the government's satisfaction and won a follow-on five-year contract that produced $168 million in revenue. Building on that success, the firm created a wholly owned subsidiary devoted exclusively to government work. Within four years, the new subsidiary had a portfolio of five-year contracts worth a total of more than $1 billion.

- A small engineering firm that had built a successful government business had grown to annual revenue of $22 million. Then the mission of the agencies in its defense weapons market changed radically and revenue began to plummet. At $17 million, managers transformed the firm to align with their client's new mission, and four years later were up to annual revenue of $54 million.

- A technology and management consulting firm had both commercial and government clients. Its new contract win rate in the government sector was less than 30 percent and, in some years, as low as 20 percent. That forced managers into a corner where they often submitted four proposals to win one new contract -- wasting the meager business development budget. So they pivoted by sharpening their business development approach, and within two years they were up to a consistent 60 percent to 65 percent win rate on proposals submitted for full and open competitive procurements.

Key Topics
- Revenue Growth Examples
- Lessons Learned
- Revenue Growth Model - Five-Year Contract
- Self Assessment

Revenue Growth Examples

Revenue Growth for Government Contractors presents approaches, tools, methods and ideas that have been used to successfully achieve consistent long-term revenue growth and may be adopted and adapted to fit the specific situation of most firms seriously interested in revenue growth.

- Facing a highly dissatisfied government client, a military products manufacturer was forced to undergo contract recompetition. Following our diagnosis, it initiated an intense strategic effort that changed the "value delivery strategy" from PRODUCT to SOLUTION (see Chapter Two for more on the strategy), rebuilt the client relationship, and won the procurement that had been designed to replace it with a competitor. The contract was worth more than $2.6 billion.

- A wholly owned subsidiary with annual revenue of $9 million reinvented itself to adopt a "solution value delivery strategy" aligned with rapidly changing requirements in its market. The result: Four consecutive years of revenue growth between 35 percent and 45 percent, producing well over $40 million in the most recent year.

- An established manufacturing company that had been doing business for more than 100 years diversified into the government market, adopted the ClientView method and grew annual revenue from $30 million to well over $100 million in less than three and a half years.

Lessons Learned

Here is what we learned from those examples that can help a government contractor grow business:

- Revenue growth results from turning a well-prepared and carefully focused strategic plan into reality.
- Emerging government markets where spending is increasing are likely to be sources of greater revenue.
- Growth firms get that way by responding to their clients' or prospects' most pressing issues.
- Agile reinvention is mandatory -- not just a good idea worth investigating, but mandatory -- to align with changes in a client's mission and/or shifts in government policies and spending.
- Develop -- and stick with -- a rigorous and disciplined business development and investment process.
- You're succeeding if you have a 50 percent or higher win rate for full and open competitive procurements. For set-aside contract, aim for 65 percent.
- Pursue and win multi-year contracts.

One attractive feature of the government market is the multi-year contract. For a simplified example, see the hypothetical revenue growth of FIRM below. It assumes just one new five-year contract win each year to build a portfolio of multiple five-year contracts. In the real world where revenue is not hypothetical, small- and medium-size companies frequently see revenue grow 25 percent to 40 percent over several years.

The revenue shown in Figure 1.1 was the result of a deliberate business development strategy.

Of course, five-year contracts, as in this example, are not the only option. Many government contracts, such as recent State Department ones for program monitoring and evaluation, go for only three years and are worth around $5 million apiece. Each firm must know its market well enough to align revenue expectations with the value and duration of typical contracts.

*Figure 1.1 **Example of FIRM's revenue growth***

Year	Annual Revenue of Legacy Market	Contract Wins in New Market	Period od Performance of New Contract	Total Annual Revenue	% Revenue Growth
1	$9,560,000	$6,000,000	5 years	$10,760,000	13%
2	$8,930,000	$13,300,000	5 years	$12,770,000	19%
3	$6,740,000	$22,400,000	5 years	$15,060,000	18%
4	$3,860,000	$32,600,000	5 years	$18,700,000	24%
5	$1,909,000	$44,900,000	5 years	$25,729,000	38%
6	$0	$48,200,000	5 years	$32,260,000	25%
7	$0	$39,000,000	5 years	$37,420,000	16%
8	$0	$56,000,000	5 years	$44,140,000	18%
9	$0	$89,000,000	5 years	$55,420,000	26%
10	$0	$104,000,000	5 years	$67,240,000	21%

FIRM's business was both commercial and government, and it had built a small business with annual revenue of about $9.6 million. But in annual business plan/strategy analysis and meetings, the owners concluded that the commercial market was declining or even dying, and offered marginal opportunities for growth. So they began to search for diversification possibilities with an eye to revenue growth. Their conclusion: Try to expand their government market into new programs needing contractors with FIRM's capabilities. Their existing government clients would be a clear asset, providing the required past performance record and proven capabilities. The stretch would be winning new contracts while shifting everything to the new market.

So FIRM focused at the start on subcontractor opportunities and small business set-aside procurements. The first year it signed on as a subcontractor on large prime contracts, establishing a five-year annual revenue average of $1.2 million. The second year FIRM captured more subcontractor positions and added $2.6 million to annual revenue. Then in the third year came the first prime contract -- a five-year, $22.4 million deal with revenue averaging $4.5 million per annum.

Meanwhile, during those three years FIRM's old business continued to produce revenue, but at a rapidly declining rate. Yet that didn't

Self Assessment Review

keep FIRM, with its focus on business development via five-year contracts and a disciplined process, from achieving annual revenue growth of 13 percent to 38 percent every year for ten years.

- Can your firm analyze active contracts and determine the average value and period of performance as well as estimates of the highest and lowest annual revenue levels over the next five years?
- Can your firm determine the new contract win rate for each month over the past three years?
- Can your firm create a five-year revenue projection based on your current win rate, with the same number of proposal submissions each year as your current practice?
- Can your firm adjust some factors in the projection to show a more aggressive revenue growth rate?
- What are the three most significant benefits your firm would get by increasing revenue over the next ten years?
- What are the three biggest obstacles to achieving that higher revenue growth rate?
- Who, in your firm, would support high revenue growth as one of no more than three strategic objectives?
- Who would resist making revenue growth a strategic objective?
- What are the three most important developments for your firm to establish revenue growth as one of your most important strategic objectives?

Remember the symbol for each letter - there will be a test later.

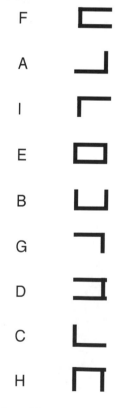

F

A

I

E

B

G

D

C

H

The test is on page 30

The answer (Big Picture) is on page 52

Don't peek

STRUCTURE AND CULTURE

Stratford Tegy, Opie Ratons, and Marten Muniman adopted the ClientView Method as the roadmap for FIRM. Put simply, it's a matter of running your business based on how your clients or customers see their world, especially when they decide to buy products and/or services that you can supply. That's just fine with leaders like Tegy, Ratons, and Muniman, who aspire to create and build strong organizations. But -- and this is a crucial point -- it's way out of kilter with entrepreneurs who want to build revenue rapidly and then sell the company. It's much easier for a client-centered business to build a company culture and operation with financial awards and recognition focused on the long-term contribution of employees -- creating a career advancement ladder based on value delivered to clients -- than it is for a "grow it and flip it" operation. You simply can't get there if selling the firm is the primary objective.

One single objective -- revenue growth -- is underpinned by three basic principles in the ClientView Method:

1. Transaction Value
2. Investment
3. Value Strategy

REVENUE GROWTH is the objective because growing firms are most likely to be the best places to work, with opportunities for career advancement, performance awards, and respectable returns to the investors and owners. Not surprisingly, we've also seen how firms with stagnant or declining revenue tend to have morale problems and higher employee turnover.

The first principle, transaction value, is the basis for the name of our method. We assert that the value of a transaction, a selling and buying event, is the buyer's perception of the value. While a seller may know in detail the cost of providing a product or service and the desired margin, the buyer's judgment of the value is what determines the final price. We believe a buyer's perception of value stems from three elements:

- The buyer's need
- The alternatives available to the buyer
- The risk the buyer is willing to take

Key Topics
- Three Principals
- Leadership Responsibilities
- Business Development investment Decisions
- Recognition, Promotion and Incentive Compensation
- Self Assessment Review

Three principals

1. Transaction value

If the buyer's 1) need is vital to his or her interests; 2) the alternatives to address the need are very few; or 3) the risk to the buyer is minimal, then the price may soar. On the other hand, if 1) the need is a passing fancy; 2) alternatives are readily available; or 3) the buyer's risks are high, then the price is most likely to be quite low.

The point for anyone interested in government business development is that we must focus not on our cost to produce, but rather on the nature and details of the government's need, the alternatives available for addressing the need, and the degree of risk the government is willing to accept. Simply put, we must understand the client's, or customer's, view of the transaction value. That is the fundamental basis of the ClientView Method.

2. Investment

We frequently find ourselves working with individuals and firms who view government business development as a form of gambling. This sentiment is often expressed as, "We've got some non-billable people, so let's put together a proposal, throw it over the wall, and see what happens." You can always find someone who cites an instance when that approach produced a win. But the occasional lucky win isn't the same as a proven strategy that produces consistent revenue growth. To us, business development is a firm's investment in its own future and, just like any investment, it requires wisdom, research, knowledge, and careful work to produce an acceptable return. Once you view it as such, business processes, accountability, discipline, and performance measurement fall right into place.

3. Value Strategy

The third principle is how you deliver value to your clients. We honor the findings of Michael Treacy and Fred Wiersema, who posit three business strategies for value delivery[4], which in our adaptation are:

- Product
- System
- Solution

Firms with a "product value delivery strategy" grow revenue as a direct result of research and development. They lead their markets and competitors by creating new products and services that set the trends, direction, and performance benchmarks in their sector or industry. Examples include Apple, Intel, Microsoft, and Canon.

Firms who excel at a "system value delivery strategy" count on highly efficient systems to deliver products and services, quality assurance and control, and cost minimization. They set standards for reliability and dependability and earn the trust and loyalty of their clients. Examples include Starbucks, McDonalds, Fidelity, and Dell.

Firms with a "solution value delivery strategy" strive for an intimate,

> A recent issue of Harvard Business Review announced that solution selling is dead. We have no concern or argument with that proposition as we see solution selling as a method of persuasion. Very differently, Solution Value Delivery is an approach to actually creating and delivering unique products and services that comprehensively address, and resolve, the challanges our client faces.

14

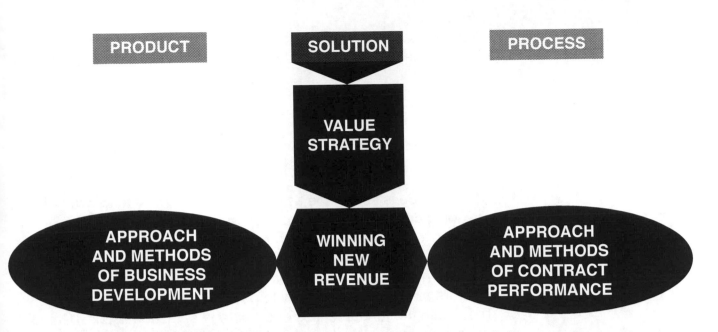

PRODUCT   **SOLUTION**   **PROCESS**

VALUE STRATEGY

APPROACH AND METHODS OF BUSINESS DEVELOPMENT

WINNING NEW REVENUE

APPROACH AND METHODS OF CONTRACT PERFORMANCE

Figure 2.1 Understanding how delivering Value to customers leads to the Value Strategy and in turn results in winning new contracts and revenue and that in turn determines the effective approaches and methods for business Development and Contract Performance

thorough, and robust understanding of their clients' objectives, challenges, and procedures to create unique solutions. See Figure 2.1. Examples include SAIC, AECOM, Booz Allen Hamilton, CACI, and Northrop Grumman.

It's no coincidence that solution providers are often the most successful government contractors. The reason: Most government procurements aim at solving or reducing the significance of a problem. Such firms' value strategy is grounded in a deep and precise understanding of the problems and obstacles their customers face, leading to unique solutions that work. Basically, that's how some small firms become large government contractors.

But firms that approach the government with a product or service and try to persuade the potential buyer that they have a solution rarely succeed. However, the methods and techniques of Solution Selling[5] are valuable to master and apply during the implementation of the positioning or capture plan.

The responsibilities of revenue growth leadership include:
- Delegation
- Business Development Investment Decisions
- Recognition, Promotion and Incentive Compensation

Revenue growth strategies succeed only as top-down initiatives. Regardless of your business title, if you're the one who controls the funds to prepare proposals, then you are the TOP and responsible for top-down implementation. Your primary responsibility is to delegate the task of winning a specific contract to one of your employees. In

Leadership Responsibilities

Delegation

general, it's a mistake to try to win a contract yourself. If there's no other choice, do it, of course. But if you can, select an individual who:

- Understands your business and/or technology.
- Has the drive and attention to detail to see pursuit of a contract through to the end.
- Has the hunger to win new business.

Now your job is asking the key questions and making key decisions, not doing business development or writing proposals. The first question, simply put: "Tell me how you are going to win this contract." What you're looking for is a fundamental strategy for winning, not a detailed plan of every little nuance. Make sure your "capture manager" knows how to put together a winning approach. Then, with the fundamentals of a strategy settled, ask this: "Could you put together a capture plan and present it to some of us for collaboration and discussion next week?"

Business Development Investment Decisions

At this point, you must have a rigorous method for making business development investment decisions. What's more, it must be transparent and unambiguous for those to whom you have entrusted business development responsibilities. And this is no time to take chances. The method you choose must be based on proven procedures and measured performance for determining your win probability.

FIRM's leaders count on four points in the process where investment decisions, or GO/NOGO decisions, are made:

1. Lead to Opportunity
2. Opportunity to Target
3. Target to Proposal
4. Proposal Pending

Each of these decision points marks a sizeable increase in funds to be invested. What's more, the four points ensure that FIRM does not stray from its time-tested business development discipline, which after all has produced a consistent win rate of at least 60 percent for full and open procurements, leading to 21.8 percent average revenue growth and providing ample funds for aggressive business development investment.

At each decision point, FIRM uses the 10-point scoring system shown in Figure 2.2 and the 60 percent win rate to evaluate win probability. The final investment decision requires a score of 80 or higher to indicate a win probability of 60 percent. If the score falls below 80, management does not fund a proposal. Time and again, their records show that the investment in proposal creation and production, while still costly, is reduced by an effective positioning or

Business Development costs must be tracked and monitored in two categories:
1. Marketing and Promotion
2. Bids and Proposals
It is imperative to have a clearly defined and consistently used demarkation between these two accounts. The first is used to position the firm, or a division, in a market niche (brochures and tradeshows) while the second is used in the pursuit of a specific contract (Capture Plan implementation and proposals).

Win Probability Assessment For Approval of Funds to Prepare Proposal SCORE OF 80 OUT OF 100 REQUIRED FOR APPROVAL TO PREPARE PROPOSAL	ALL COMPETITORS ARE LIKELY TO BE BETTER THAN US		WE ARE BETTER THAN SOME COMPETITORS		WE ARE BETTER THAN MOST COMPETITORS			WE ARE EQUAL TO THE STRONGEST COMPETITOR	WE ARE BETTER THAN THE STRONGEST COMPETITOR IN SOME ASPECTS	WE ARE BETTER THAN ALL COMPETITORS - INMATCHED

#	Criteria	1	2	3	4	5	6	7	8	9	10
1	Do we understand the prospect's challenge and have a concise plan for helping the project be successful?										
2	Does the prospect know us as a leading firm in the issues of this SOW?										
3	Does the prospect know our Project Manager and key staff as outstanding professionals?										
4	Do we and our team members have all of the capabilities required to perform successfully?										
5	Does this contract fit our strategic plan and provide strategic advantages?										
6	Can we prepare an exceptional winning proposal?										
7	Can we submit a competitive price?										
8	Can we manage or mitigate all risks of this contract?										
9	Are our Past Performance Assessments relevant and exceptional?										
10	Do we know the competition and have a plan to beat them?										
Total Score											

Figure 2.2 Business Development Investment Decision Assessment Matrix

capture plan, leading to a higher percentage of wins.

Once FIRM fashions a capture plan and follows the path of discussion, review, and approval, it's time to open a "bid and proposal" budget and account number for time sheet and expense reporting. Up to now, all time and expense charges for this lead were in the "marketing and promotion" budget item in the overhead or G&A (general and administration) accounts. The bid and proposal budget account initiation is Firm's first major decision to invest in the future of the company. The approved capture plan should reflect a compelling case for wise and prudent investment. FIRM will, of course, monitor the capture plan as it takes on a life of its own.

As FIRM nears the RFP release date, it's time to review the proposal production plan and budget that have been prepared by the capture manager and/or proposal manager. This is FIRM's second investment decision. Most of the time, proposal preparation will cost more than actually bringing the capture plan into being. So FIRM makes sure that the capture plan and strategy to win are on track and will lead to a successful proposal.

FIRM's final, or fourth, decision is to review and approve the technical and price proposals. Once approved, submit the bid or proposal to the prospective client.

Recognition, Promotion and Incentive Compensation

CEOs struggle to navigate the challenge of incentive compensation, but nowhere are waters choppier than with business development professionals. Poorly designed incentive compensation or pay-for-performance programs often result in disincentives and decreased performance.

The dilemma for incentive compensation involves:

- Widespread acceptance of incentive compensations as a fundamental part of a compensation package.
- Equally widespread documentation of the many failures of incentive compensations.
- Excessive reliance on money to motivate performance while paying little attention to other powerful motivational factors such as power, respect, team acceptance, and rectitude.

Incentive compensation is not required for government contractors, but, if used, must be presented in the Cost Accounting Standards disclosure to the Defense Contracting Audit Agency (DCAA, which supplies contract audit services to many government agencies, not just Defense). If a firm has an incentive compensation program it must be designed correctly, or DCAA may rule that it is actually profit-sharing and therefore not an allowable cost in either overhead or G&A.

One of the most difficult areas to apply incentive compensation or pay for performance is business development in the government marketplace -- that is, aligning incentives with the objective of revenue growth. The reason is simple. Winning government contracts requires a team effort over an extended time and business development and contract execution are often highly integrated activities that involve many different individuals.

What's more, the time from spotting a new business opportunity to

Performance Situation	Employee we want to incentivize
Claire inherited the management responsibility for an IDIQ contract and significantly improved performance and client satisfaction resulting in an increase in annual revenue from $200K to $1.5M. However, the original expectation was that this contract would produce $3M in annual revenue. Claire has previously been ineffective at winning new contracts.	**Claire Smith** **Project Manager**
Brian led the effort in marketing and proposal creation resulting in winning a new $100M/Five Year IDIQ contract in a new strategically important market sector. Revenue is expected to begin in about four months. Brian is not going to manage the project.	**Brian Bolt** **Capture Manager**
Sarah developed market intelligence, assembled the team of sub-contractors, and created win themes for a successful proposal resulting in winning a firm fixed priced contract valued at $8M and scheduled for completion in 18 months. However, Sarah did not work on the actual proposal due to reassignment.	**Sarah Jones** **Business Development Manager**
Judith produced a brilliant proposal with minimal staff support and an unusually short schedule. This proposal resulted in winning a significant Cost Plus contract with a repeat client who has been very pleased with the company's past performance. However, Judith had nothing to do with the high level of past performance satisfaction	**Judith Power** **Proposal Manager**

Figure 2.3 Typical Performance Situations With Incentive Compensation Complexities

contract award and revenue actually hitting the books is frequently many months and can be several years. So the team that brought in the win may have a variety of leaders and participants, perhaps even changing all personnel during the long procurement process. The challenges are:

- Aligning the incentive plan with the overarching corporate strategy.
- Matching incentive performance criteria with the employee's responsibilities.
- Fitting the incentive plan to the drawn-out acquisition process or cycle of federal contracting.
- Fitting the incentive program within DCAA parameters.
- Aligning incentives and revenue growth strategy.

The vignettes in Figure 2.3 describe a few typical situations that could take place in a single firm. Claire, Brian, Sarah, and Judith are all making valuable contributions to the company's success. Their stories illustrate the difficulty of creating a fair incentive program. Key factors in their individual achievements are really the result of others' work. Plus, only Claire is actually earning and growing revenue; yet she did nothing to win the contract. Brian, Sarah, and Judith have all won contracts that will earn revenue in the future, but not right now.

Further, the revenue potential of each new contract is quite different.

Sarah's new contract immediately becomes backlog in that the total contract value is authorized at contract execution. Brian's new contract might produce $20 million annually for the next five years, but that's a big "might." Judith clearly gets credit for a good proposal, but the win is based largely on the firm's reputation, which was established by the work of others. So as you can see, designing an incentive system that fairly rewards performance in a variety of complex situations is no easy matter.

Some mistakes

"Bounty" systems, or sales commissions, for business development are incentive pay packages for "salesmen" strongly linked to winning new contracts or task orders. But as companies delve into business development, complexity increases and distortions grow. Bounties overlook team effort, do not account for the long time span of the marketing and sales effort, and must be contrived economically to accommodate the lack or small amount of revenue available at contract award. When the contract won is IDIQ (indefinite duration/ indefinite quantity), the concept of a bounty incentive is difficult to defend. Further, awarding bounty incentive compensation is often perceived as inequitable, and team participants lose incentive.

"Ad hoc" incentives can meet the needs of a temporary problem or a disgruntled employee. Yet in some cases, management mistakenly believes that the ad hoc incentive is a private matter between the affected employee and themselves. Not likely. Instead, peer employees excluded from the incentive tend to believe that they have been treated unfairly, and the incentive to perform fritters away. Further, such incentives may become audit issues when DCAA reviews overhead and G&A rates.

That does not mean that incentive compensation for business development should be eliminated. The practice of pay for performance is far too widespread in American business to deny employees a benefit they see as an entitlement. Rather, firms must devise incentives programs that recognize team effort, the lengthy government procurement process, and the economic realities of often minimal revenue during the first three months after award and of revenue flow spread over several years of contracting. The best ways to reward consistent performers in this area are combinations of recognition awards, promotions, titles, and salary increases with expanded responsibilities (and, of course, some incentive and/or equity compensation).

Meeting the challenge

It is important to devise a creative incentive program that includes a pay-for-performance program adjusted to the time span of government procurement and the numerous individual efforts it takes to win. It should be integrated with other motivational factors such as recognition, awards, and increases of responsibility (promotion). Many government contractors recommend leveraging the firm's equity or various forms of employee ownership in the firm.

Simple systems with clear metrics are likely to be more effective than complex scoring structures or algorithms that only a few in management could really grasp. Incentives that include generous individual and team recognition, career advancement, realistic financial reward, and possibly equity can be far more effective than incentive compensation alone. To put it simply, reward the team for effort over a long procurement cycle using a straightforward framework that includes all employees.

FIRM devised an incentive system that included all employees/ stakeholders broken down into six levels for one or more of 10 types of recognitions or awards. The two elements -- employees/ stakeholders and recognition/awards -- are defined below. It worked so well that the leaders credited it with creating and maintaining the desired company culture.

Below is a list of the eligible levels and the types of recognition or awards provided for each and a summary is shown in Figure 2.4:

1. Letters of Commendation -- Consultants and 1099 staff augmentation personnel may get letters of commendation from practice leaders or business unit managers and even executives when performance merits. It is understood that the letters may be used as references for their other clients or customers.

2. Victory Parties -- The day FIRM is notified of a contract win it hosts a party for the proposal and capture teams and any other employees who participated in the business development effort and are available. Senior management speaks briefly about the award's impact on FIRM's future and gives each team member a performance memento, a small stuffed bear, which grew out of the nickname "Bear Hunters" for proposal teams and other contributors. Most employees display the teddy bears on a shelf in their work area. The capture manager and proposal manager recognize individual team members and thank everyone for their contribution. FIRM provides food and refreshment. The parties usually start at 4 p.m. and are over by 6 p.m. There are no monetary awards at these events.

3. Individual Spot Awards -- Business unit managers have the authority and budget to issue spot awards within a week after a staffer's exceptional performance in line with FIRM's strategic objectives. The business unit manager briefly describes the achievement in writing for executive management and the staff member. Most often, project managers or key contributors recommend awards -- $200 and the teddy bear -- to the business unit manager. These awards were also made public during the Monthly Nominated Awards meeting and newsletter.

4. Monthly Nominated Awards -- Any FIRM employee, including a

FIRM's System

Recognitions / Awards

supervisor, can nominate a staff member for a monthly nominated award by submitting a written statement (less than one page) to the CEO. The CEO, COO, and CFO then rank and select the awardees. An annual budget provides awards for up to three percent of the staff each month, consisting of $200 and a teddy bear performance memento. Awards are made at a brief monthly meeting of all employees, where the CEO reads the nomination and asks each awardee to come forward. The nomination statements for each awardee and similar information on each spot award, along with comments from the CEO, are distributed each month in the newsletter.

5. Quarterly Awards -- Project managers and key contributors (at FIRM senior technical experts not involved in management functions are called key contributors) are evaluated quarterly for their performance compared with FIRM's strategic objectives. This category includes both direct (billable labor to contracts) and indirect (labor in overhead and G&A categories) personnel. Evaluation factors include:

- Client or customer letters of commendation about individuals and/or FIRM performance under a contract.
- Performance that improves the financial position by reducing overhead costs, achieving objectives under budget, and increasing contract revenue.
- Leadership and contributions critical to the award of new contracts.
- Performance exceeding an individual's specific performance objectives.
- Leadership contributions that enhance FIRM's reputation and market position via enhanced or expanded capabilities, as well as recognition or awards that improve FIRM's reputation and market position.
- Other contributions to FIRM's annual and long-term strategic objectives.

The budget and size of the incentive pool is set annually and may be adjusted during the fiscal year to align with revenue. The value of the pool and the budget is confidential, known only to the CEO, COO, and CFO.

6. Annual Awards -- Business unit managers and executives are evaluated annually regarding FIRM's achievement of strategic objectives, including profit. The category includes both corporate and profit center management. Performance evaluation factors are:

- Achievement of revenue growth objective by each business unit and the company.
- Achievement of gross profit growth objectives by each business unit and the company.

- Achievement of business development goals by each business unit and the company.

The Board of Directors meets at the end of each fiscal year and determines the incentives for the CEO, COO, and CFO.

7. Promotion -- Promotion with increased responsibility, appropriate title change, and pay increases requires evaluation of several performance factors, including helping FIRM grow revenue.

8. Equity Distributions -- All employees are eligible for equity (company shares of stock) distributions based on position and performance. Again, contributions to revenue growth play a prominent role in equity distribution decisions. All require Board approval with documentation for the amount of the distribution and the performance of each recipient.

Incentive pools for items 2, 3, 4, 5, and 6 are established annually. They may be adjusted to align with actual revenue. The amounts are carried in the budget chart of accounts as compensation in overhead and/or G&A.

9. Profit Sharing -- All equity owners are eligible for profit sharing through dividends. However, FIRM has not issued any dividends and has no plans to do so in the immediate future, as all earnings are pumped into aggressive revenue growth.

10. Change-in-Control Contracts -- The Board of Directors can select individuals within FIRM to receive contracts that ensure their

Figure 2.4 Incentive Plan Matrix

INCENTIVE	1099s & Consultants	STAFF	Project Managers & Key Contributors	Business Unit Managers	Excutives	Owners
1. Letters of Commendation						
2. Victory Parties						
3. Individual Spot Awards						
4. Monthly Nominated Awards						
5. Quarterly Awards						
6. Annual Awards						
7. Promotion						
8. Equity Distributions						
9. Profit Sharing						
10. Change in Control Contracts						

position and compensation if the company changes hands. The Board determines the terms, conditions, and financial provisions for change-in-control contracts, and creates agreements to benefit FIRM.

Employees / Stakeholders

Eligible groups – Consultants/Temp Staff/Employees/Owners

A. 1099s and consultants
B. Staff
C. Project managers and key contributors
D. Business unit managers
E. Executives
F. Owners

Measuring Individual Business Dvelopment Performance

An example of the approach that FIRM used to collaborate with project managers, key contributors, business unit managers and executives to establish performance metrics is shown in Figure 2.5 below. In this case, the document is for the position of Director of Business Development. The employee holding this position

Figure 2.5 Example of FIRM Performance Metrics for Director of Business Development

Responsibility	Work to be Performed	Metric	Threshold	Objective
Revenue Growth	Lead effort to consistently increase revenue	Percent growth of annual revenue	20% annual revenue growth	32% revenue growth this year
Market Position	Annual Marketing Plan	Approved plan and budget		
Market Position	Internal and external communication of annual Marketing Plan and status	Commitment of FIRM managers to Annual Marketing Plan	FIRM BD personnel and BU managers fully understandand are committed to Annual Marketing Plan	Response of BD and BUs to adverse events keeps Plan objectives on track
Market Position	Public relations and media communication	Number and nature of published articles about FIRM	One published major article on FIRM	Five published major articles on FIRM
Market Position	Communication channels including website, brochures, conferences, advertising, etc.	Web site hits by government organizations, specific results achieved at conferences, customer response to marketing collateral	Web site hits by government offices consistently increase	Number of website hits doubles last year's total
Market Position	Support of all business units" market positioning activities	Annual Performance Assessment by FIRM BU Managers and business development personnel	FIRM BU managers satisfied with business development performance	Firm BU managers rate marketing performance as exceptional

Responsibility	Work to be Performed	Metric	Threshold	Objective
Business Development Funnel	Annual Sales Plan	Approved plan and budget	Annual Plan achieved to meet threshold	Achievement of all objectives defined in Annual Marketing and Sales Plan
Business Development Funnel	Development and implementation of Business Development tracking, forecasting, and performance measurement	Accuracy and timeliness of funnel information, reliability of revenue forecasts for new contracts, win/loss rate in value and number percentages	Funnel data updated monthly. New contract information provided by FIRM business developers, sales engineers, and capture managers, 45% win rate for new competitive contracts	65% win rate for new competive contracts
Business Development Funnel	Creation and management of Strategic Advisory Council	Creating and maintaining a group of senior retired officers and former government managers and executives as effective "Insider Advisors" and "Door Openers"	The sources for 60% of this year's revenue are represented in the Strategic Advisory Council	The sources for 80% of this years's revenue are represented in the Strategic Advisory Council
Business Development Funnel	Management and Chair of Business Development Council	Monthly FIRM Business Development Council meetings	Participation by all capture managers, BU managers, proposal managers at every meeting	Participation by all capture managers, BU managers, proposal managers at every meeting
Business Development Funnel	Chair and facilitate "Bid Board"	Monthly Bid Board meetings. Effective bid / No Bid decisions	Participation by CEO, BU managers and capture managers at every meeting	Participation by CEO, BU managers and capture managers at every meeting
Business Development Funnel	Oversee Capture Planning	Capture Plans for strategically significant qualified targets	50% of strategically significant qualified targets have approved capture plans	80% of strategically significant qualified targets have approved capture plans
Business Development Funnel	Pricing information development	Legally providing accurate and reliable competitive pricing information	Current information in database for all 1st Tier competitors	Current information in database for all 1st Tier and 2nd Tier competitors
Business Development Funnel	Manage proposal creation and production process	Total and average proposal cost	Stabilize and maintain cost of proposal production	Reduce, stabilize and maintain cost of proposal production

Responsibility	Work to be Performed	Metric	Threshold	Objective
Business Development Funnel	Contract negotiation support	Documentation of support provided	Support as requested	Support as requested
Business Development Resources	Business Development resource planning, forecasting and management	Network of internal and external resources and workload forecasting system	80% of Business Development workload forecast 3 weeks in advance	90% of Business Development workload forecast 6 weeks in advance
Business Development Resources	Management of external Business Development proposal writers, graphic artists, consultants, and related human resources	Create and maintain a network of proven, reliable and relevant external resources at reasonable rates	At least 50% of external resources have prior successful experience with the specific prospective client on major proposals	At least 80% of external resources have prior successful experience with the specific prospective client on major proposals
Business Development Resources	Management of Business Development tools, services, and related resources	Obtain and maintain computers, software, and other systems for BD	Only minor schedule slippage due to equipment	No schedule slippage due to equipment
Business Development Resources	Management of proposal information database (resumes, project descriptions, standard texts, and SAM information) and proposal repository	Create and maintain archive and database of BD information and data	All major proposals in archive and BD database	All proposals in archive and database and retrievable by proposal and by subject matter
Business Development Resources	Management of customer information database and directory	Create and maintain the customer information database	Key decision makers/ influencers of major client organizations in database	Key decision makers/ influencers of all client organizations in database
Business Development Resources	Management of competitor information database and directory	Create and maintain the competitor information database	Major competitors in data base	All competitors in database
Key Client Program	Develop Annual Key Account Management Plan focused on the top 20% of clients (measured by annual revenue)	Approved plan and budget	Annual Plan prepared and approved	Achievement of all objectives defined in Annual Key Client Program Plan
Key Client Program	Develop a client specific relationship plan that achieves: 1.Client view of FIRM as a firm that makes key contributions to mission achievement and success	A. Key client revenue growth. B. SAM Past Performance and other assessments of FIRM performance. C. Repeat client revenue growth.	A. Satisfactory assessments by Business Unit Management and Program Manager. B. Key Client revenue increases 20% each year.	Repeat Key Client annual revenue growth exceeds 35%

Responsibility	Work to be Performed	Metric	Threshold	Objective
Key Client Program	2. Client comfort in sharing their program and internal concerns with FIRM	Same as above	Same as above	Same as above
Key Client Program	3. FIRM viewed by client as critical to client's future plans	Same as above	Same as above	Same as above
Key Client Program	4. FIRM as a source of important information to client regarding program status and trends	Same as above	Same as above	Same as above
Key Client Program	5. FIRM viewed by client as the easiest firm to work and collaborate with	Same as above	Same as above	Same as above
Key Client Program	6. Client revenue increasing each year	Same as above	Same as above	Same as above
Key Client Program	7. Client going out of their way to support FIRM	Same as above	Same as above	Same as above
Leadership	Leadership within FIRM	Peer recognition	Recognition in Peer Performance Evaluations	Recognition in Peer Performance Evaluations
Leadership	Leadership within Business development Group	Peer and subordinate recognition	Recognition in subordinate Performance Evaluations	Recognition in subordinate Performance Evaluations
Leadership	Mentoring of supervised employees	Employee career growth	Mentoring program established in BD	Examples of leadership and career growthcareer

and his immediate supervisor review each responsibility, the work to be performed, the applicable metric, the minimal or threshold performance required and the objective performance level that FIRM's strategy requires.

Weights, or values, are assigned to each of the six responsibilities to define the proportion of the annual incentive that is to be awarded for each responsibility:

Revenue Growth - 40%
Market Position - 10%
Business Development Funnel - 10%
Business Development Resources - 10%
Key Client Program - 20%
Leadership - 10%

Self Assessment Review

- What are the underlying principles that shape the philosophy and culture of your firm?
- Are they clearly understood by most of the management and staff?
- Is your firm's revenue growth strategy visibly driven from the very top position in your firm?
- Does your firm manage business development as an investment process or a matter of getting lucky?
- Does your firm's recognition and incentive compensation program include all employees?
- Is the recognition and incentive compensation program generally understood by all employees?
- Does your firm's recognition and incentive compensation program clearly align with the firm's strategic objectives?
- Is your firm's recognition and incentive compensation program a critical component in creating, building, and maintaining the firm's culture?

BUSINESS DEVELOPMENT FRAMEWORK

As stated earlier, FIRM operates under the direction of its three founders and owners:

- Stratford Tegy, President and CEO, often referred to as Strategy
- Opie Ratons, COO, often referred to as Operations
- Marten Muniman, CFO, often referred to as Money

Several years after they launched the company, a proposal writing effort brought their growing conflicts and misunderstandings to a head. The employee managing the proposal brought a draft section to Strategy, who made changes, deleting and adding text. The proposal manager edited the text and took it to Operations for review. She also made changes, deleting and adding. Again, the proposal manager edited the text and took it to Money, who also deleted and added. Finally, the proposal manager took it back to Strategy for final approval. Strategy didn't like it. The text he had added was either gone or had been changed in a big way, and included text additions he had not approved. So he blamed the proposal manager, who, within a few weeks, resigned and joined a competing firm.

Meanwhile, revenue growth was at an unacceptably low level.

The problem, which the three leaders eventually recognized, had two major components:

A poorly designed review and approval process that was harming many of the firm's business activities, not just proposals.
Real and significant disagreements between the three leaders.

As they looked into the problem, a haphazard approach to proposals emerged as the culprit. They found that they were making spending decisions for business development based on:

- Availability of employees who were not currently billable.
- Quid pro quo obligations to other firms with whom they had teamed on previous procurements.
- An attitude that submitting proposals was similar to playing the lottery.
- A standoff in which one leader was eager to propose while the other two were reluctant to disagree.

Key Topics
- The Big Picture
- Framework
- Business Development Responsibilities
- Self Assessment Review

Frequently, they were deciding to prepare and submit a proposal after they learned that an RFP had been issued. To make matters worse, they rarely knew who the primary competitors were, and in most cases had never talked with anyone in the prospective client's organization.

The Big Picture

That's when they decided to develop and adhere to a shared vision[6], or Big Picture, for business development. Then they could find out if a similar approach would work for other business processes.

How to test the "Big Picture" concept and see for yourself if it makes sense.

See page 12 for the test data

1. A table a few pages back asked you to remember letters and symbols for a test.
2. This is that test.
3. Draw the symbol for each letter in the space to the left. Do not look back for the table. Do this from your memory only.
4. When finished with the test, continue reading until you come to the next part of the test.

The test shows that we humans, when presented with a number of apparently disconnected data points or bits of information, struggle to make sense of the data. But when we have a "Big Picture," we can almost instantaneously fit the data into a coherent message or pattern. Basically, we have four possible outcomes when confronted with new data or information:

- You learn nothing worth noting from the new data or information because you do not possess a relevant "Big Picture."
- You learn something and I do not because you have a relevant "Big Picture" and I have none.
- You and I both learn something from the new data or information, but we learn different, possibly conflicting things because we have different "Big Pictures."
- You and I both learn the same thing because we share a relevant "Big Picture."

The odds are that the last outcome is the most efficient and productive for a business like FIRM if the shared "Big Picture" is based on reality, results in pragmatic conclusions, and produces practical actions.

Businesses like FIRM have managers and staff working with clients and customers every day. And every day, those people are exposed to bits of data and information relevant to business development. But in many firms, if you ask about business development, nearly all the employees will tell you they have nothing to do with it. They believe this occurs because they have no shared framework of FIRM's business development approach that requires or values the information they are failing to capture.

As you can see on the following page in Figure 3.1, FIRM's business development framework is a poster-sized matrix of columns and rows. The 10 columns define the major time periods in business development, starting with the client or customer recognizing a need and ending with execution of a contract. The 10 rows are major elements in the business process.

Time Elements are the column titles across the top of the matrix. The column titles are Strategy, Niche Needs, Market Position, Prospecting, Positioning, Transitioning, Proposal, and Contract Execution. The column on the far right presents the value of the actions described in the rows. The duration of the time elements in this framework approximate the durations in the government's time elements for an acquisition. See the 16 Acquisition Scenarios in Chapter 6 for a detailed example of the government's acquisition process.

Business Process Elements are the row titles listed down the far left column. The titles are Client or Customer Events, Timeline, Strategic Objective, Tactical Objective, Milestones, Metrics, Phase and Task Responsibilities. Capabilities, Standards, and Procedures that FIRM uses are described in Chapter Five, Business Development Management.

This framework provide a shared business development vision for all of FIRM's managers and staff. Further, it created a FIRM specific vocabulary for discussing business development issues and decision making. These attributes alone help eliminate misunderstanding and wasted effort from business development activities. When fully implemented with the following Figure 3.2 Business Development Responsibilities, the framework improves efficiency and reduces costs.

Business Development Framework

Figure 3.1	1	2	3	4
FIRM BD FRAMEWORK	**STRATEGY**	**NICHE NEEDS**	**MARKET POSITION**	**PROSPECTING**
GOVERNMENT ACTIONS	Determine Need, Validate Funding	Acquisition Planning, Assign Buyer / Contract Specialist	Market Research, Conduct Market Survey	Pre-Solicitation Contact with Potential Offerors
TIME LINE	**-3 YEARS**	**-2.6 YEARS**	**-2.3 YEARS**	**-1.7 YEARS**
STRATEGIC OBJECTIVES	**Identify** and define FIRM strategic objectives and target markets **Align** FIRM organization with strategic objectives	Understand the objectives, plans and needs of Government organizations within Strategic Market Niches	Place useful, valuable and persuasive information with decision makers and influencers in TARGET MARKET NICHES and legacy markets	Find and qualify specific business opportunities within TARGET MARKET NICHES and legacy market
TACTICAL OBJECTIVES	**Annual** Strategic Plan **Annual** Business Plan **Annual** Marketing Plan **Annual** Sales Plan	**Who's** buying, what are they buying, why are they buying, who are they buying from, how much are they spending **Trend** Analysis of Strategic Market niches **Refine** prioitization of market niches **Identify** key decsion makers	**Define** "useful, valuable and persuasive" in FIRM market context **Develop** and implement multi-channel marketing & communication program **Establish** "inside information network"	Within TARGET and legacy market niches, identify and qualify opportunities with prospect's mission, SOO, SOW and contract value sufficient to achieve or exceed strategic revenue growth objectives
MILESTONES	**Annual** Planning Retreat **Approval** of the four tactical objectives	Market Niche Analysis (MNA) Needs Analysis Trends Prioritization Decision Makers	Complete implementation of Annual Marketing Plan	Sufficient qualified opportunities identified
METRICS	**Completion** and presentation of Annual Plans to FIRM Board and management **Annual** Plans communication package distributed to all employees	**Timely** completion of MNA **Clear** and precise management decision on TARGET NICHE diversication	**Response** from TARGET MARKET NICHES requesting information **Teaming** inquiries and invitations **Technical** Presentations **Website** visits by prospect organizations	Number and value of QUALIFIED OPPORTUNITIES compared to Strategic Revenue Growth Objectives
PHASE LEADER	CEO	BUMs	Marketing Manager	BD Manager
TASK LEADERS	COO, CFO, BUMS & BD Manager	BD Manager, PMs & KCs	BD Manager	CEO, BUMs & PMs or KCs

5 POSITIONIING	6 TRANSITIONING	7 PROPOSAL	8 EXECUTION	Value – Repeatable and improvable process
Develop Selection Plan	Build Solicitation	Issue Solicitation, Evaluation, Issue Award Notices,	Monitor Performance & Contract Administration, Close Out	*See Government's 16 Acquisition Scenarios for specific information*
-1.5 YEARS	**-0.6 YEARS**	**-0.5 YEARS**	**+5 YEARS**	*Spans full performance life-cycle.*
Plan and implement capture strategy to position FIRM as the firm most likely to win contract	Transfer compelling win strategy from capture effort to proposal creation and production	Create and submit a winning proposal	Perform at an assessed "EXCEPTIONAL" level	*Consistent adherence to a rational linked chain of Strategic and Tactical objectives results in consistent, long-term revenue growth. Ad-hoc, sporadic or short-term Strategic and Tactical objectives tend to result in revenue flucuation and operation instability.*
Influence prospect's acquisition process to enhance the prospect's ability to achieve their objectives **Create** the belief in the prospect's organization that FIRM is the right firm for this contract **Produce** deliverables that are critical to development of a winning proposal	**Create** a clear and compelling win strategy • Hot buttons • Discriminators • Preferences • Teaming • Price to Win **Transfer** from Capture Team to Proposal Team	**Diversification** - Win more than 50% of proposal submitted for full and open competition **Legacy** - Win more than 90% of proposals submitted **IDIQ** - Win 100% of Task Order proposals submitted under existing contracts	**Achieve**, obtain and complete client documented FIRM performance assessments at an "EXCEPTIONAL" or "EXCELLENT" level **Past** Performance Documentation **Resume** and capability documentation and updates	
Implementation of Capture Plan **Completion** of Capture Plan Deliverables **Approved** Win Strategy for Proposal	Proposal Creation & Production Management Plan drafted	Create and submit a winning proposal	Client assessment of FIRM performance	*Planned Milestones and defined performance metrics enable meaningful company and individual performance assessment in multi-year business development cycle.*
Number and value of approved Targets for Capture Plan implementation compared to Strategic Revenue Growth Objectives	Number and value of Proposal approved production compared to Strategic Revenue Growth Objectives	**Number** and value of contracts won **Win Rate** (number and value percentage) **Contract** portfolio burn rate **Proposal** cost	Quality Schedule Budget Project Management subcontractor Management Business relationship Resume updates Past Performance updates	
Capture Manager	Capture Manager & Proposal Manager	Proposal Manager & BD Manager	BUM & Project Manager	*Defined roles and responsibilities facilitates teamwork and efficiency.*
CEO, BUMs, BD Manager	CEO, BUM & BD Manager	CEO, CFO, BUM & Capture Manager	BD Manager	

Business Development Responsibilities

To complete the framework as their shared vision of business development, the three owners collaborated with managers and staff to define 112 tasks or activities during major business development pursuits. Then they assigned responsibility for each task to a position in FIRM's organization. Not only did that identify the contributors or collaborators for each task, but also who was to see the task through to completion. What the owners didn't expect was that the exercise also clarified the links between tasks performed by different people in different departments -- showing how one person's job completion affected the start of another's responsibility. Additionally, it resolved simmering turf battles while enlarging the responsibilities for many individuals.

Figure 3.2 Task / Responsibility Matrix (continues for six pages)

	TASKS	Executive	BUM	PM & KC	Staff	BD Manager	Capture Manager	Proposal Manager
A	**Processes**							
A.1	Populate FIRM Business Development Opportunity Tracking System		CC		PS	ER	CC	PS
A.2	Quarterly Marketing and Sales reviews and Action Planning	FA	CA	PS	PS	ER	CC	CC
A.3	Periodic Business Development Coordination Meetings		CC			ER	CC	CC
A.4	Preparing Annual Strategic / Business Plan	FA	ER	PS	PS	CC	PS	PS
A.5	Alignment of FIRM organization, systems and processes with strategic plan and objectives	ER	CC	PS	PS	PS	PS	PS
A.6	Improvement of Business Development Processes, Guidance, and Templates	FA	PS		PS	ER	CC	CC
A.7	Monthly assessment and report of Business Development Performance	FA	CC			ER	PS	PS
B	**Develop BD Strategy**							
B.1	Annual FIRM Strategy	FA						
B.2	Annual FIRM Business Plan	FA						
B.3	Target Strategic Markets	CA	ER			CC		
B.4	Establish Pursuit Criteria and Filter procedure for selecting new opportunities		CC			ER	PS	
B.5	Establish BD Discipline (BD Framework)					ER	PS	PS
B.6	Conduct BD Training					ER	PS	PS
B.7	BD operational coordination, workload forecast and management, and performance management		CC	PS	PS	ER	PS	PS
B.8	Strategic Market Niche Needs Analysis		CC		PS	ER		
B.9	Annual Market survey to identify candidate diversification paths		CC			ER		

TASKS	Executive	BUM	PM & KC	Staff	BD Manager	Capture Manager	Proposal Manager
B.10 Rank candidate diversification paths by revenue potential and risk to FIRM and identify obstacles to success		CC	PS	PS	ER	PS	
B.11 Meet with key executives in Target Market Niches		CA			ER		
B.12 Present Strategic Market Niche Analysis to Excutives and BUMs		ER			CC		
B.13 Select Strategic Market Niches for development and develop Action Plan	FA						
C Marketing							
C.1 Develop Internal Sales Support Capability		CC			ER	CC	
C.2 Marketing Collateral & Website				PS	ER		
C.3 Media Relations for Press Releases				PS	ER		
C.4 Conferences and Trade Shows	PS	CC			ER	CC	
C 5 FIRM Branding	FA			PS	ER		
C.6 Memberships and Professional Societies	CA	ER					
C.7 Collect, compile and use awards, performance assessments and client commendations		CC	CC		ER		
C.8 Speakers Bureau	CC	CC	CC		ER		
C.9 Pre-Strategize by market and competitor		ER			CC		
C.10 Key Client Management Plan		ER			CC		
C.11 Target prospects and prepare account plan		ER			CC	CC	
D Find and Qualify Specific Opportunities							
D.1 Identify opportunities	CC	ER	CC		ER	CC	
D.2 Opportunities with current clients		ER	CC				
D.3 Opportunities with new prospects					ER	CC	
D.4 Opportunities with teaming partners	CC	ER	CC				
D.5 Opportunities under existing contracts - IDIQ Task Orders		CC	ER				
D.6 Opportunities in Tracking Services				PS	ER		
D.7 Identify and assign FIRM Opportunity Champion		ER			CC		
D.8 Gather information to Qualify or Dismiss Opportunity					CA	ER	
D.9 Enter opportunity data into FIRM BD Tracking System						ER	
D.10 Obtain intelligence, objectives, cost ceiling and probable competitor information						ER	
D.11 Assess Opportunity fit ti FIRM Strategic Objectives		CA			CA	ER	
D.12 Nominate Opportunity for promotion to Qualified Opportunity						ER	

TASKS	Executive	BUM	PM & KC	Staff	BD Manager	Capture Manager	Proposal Manager
D.13 Approve Qualified Opportunity	FA	CC			CC	CC	
E **Develope Capture Plan**							
E.1 Assign Capture Manager and core team		ER			CC		
E.2 Gather Capture Plan information						ER	
E.3 Determine the precise mission or purpose of the contract						ER	
E.4 Determine elements or factors critical to the contract's success						ER	
E.5 Determine prospect's major concerns regarding contract success						ER	
E.6 Determine consequences or impacts of contract not being performed successfully						ER	
E.7 Determine prospect's vision of the ideal contract performance						ER	
E.8 Determine names and roles of persons likely to influence selection of contract winner						ER	
E.9 Draft Capture Plan		CC			CC	ER	
E.10 Obtain information about type of contract, contract value, and Period of Performance						ER	
E.11 Obtain information about procurement schedule, RFP issue date, Proposal due date and Contract award date						ER	
E.12 Obtain information about Program History; previous program contracts, firms involved in program, incumbents, funding history or situation, and major events						ER	
E.13 Obtain names, positions, phone numbers, addresses, and potential role of individuals involved in selection process						ER	
E.14 Identify major competitors, role (prime or sub), strengths and weaknesses						ER	
E.15 Analyze competitors in comparison with anticipated scope of work						ER	
E.16 Analyze strengths and weaknesses of competitive teams						ER	
E.17 Determine price to win						ER	
E.18 Create teaming strategy and criteria		CC			CC	ER	
E.19 Analyze corporate risk and mitigations	FA					ER	
E.20 Prepare discriminator analyses		CC			CC	ER	
E.21 Determine win strategy		CC			CC	ER	
E.22 Develop Capture Plan Action Plan						ER	

TASKS		Executive	BUM	PM & KC	Staff	BD Manager	Capture Manager	Proposal Manager
E.23	Review and approve capture plan	FA	CA			CA		
E.24	Nominate OPPORTUNITY FOR PROMOTION TO QUALIFIED TARGET – Approve B&P Account						ER	
E.25	Approve QUALIFIED TARGET	FA	CA			CA		
E.26	Open Bid and Proposal cost tracking account number						ER	
F	**Implement Capture Plan**							
F.1	Attend Industry Day						ER	
F.2	Collaborate on Value proposition		CC			CC	CC	
F.3	Identify Teaming candidates		CC			CC	ER	
F.4	Initiate teaming relationships		CC			CC	ER	
F.5	Negotiate Teaming Agreements		ER			PS	CC	
F.6	Prepare Capture Plan Deliverables						ER	
F.7	Update Capture Plan						ER	
F.8	Prepare mock up of executive summary						ER	
F.9	Confirm/Assign proposal core team		CC			ER	CC	CC
F.10	Review lessons learned from previous proposals					CC	CC	ER
F.11	Define baseline solution to accomplish prospect's objectives & adjust price to win					CC	ER	CC
F.12	Prepare draft proposal management plan					CC	CC	ER
F.13	Plan Kick Off meeting					CC	CC	ER
F.14	Nominate QUALIFIED TARGET for promotion to PROPOSAL IN PROCESS						ER	
F.15	Approve PROPOSAL IN PROCESS	FA						
F.16	Receive RFP		CC			CC	CC	ER
G	**Create, Produce and Submit Proposal**							
G.1	Prepare Proposal Management Plan with outline, schedule, assignments and other information							ER
G.2	Hold Proposal Kick Off Meeting							ER
G.3	Prepare Annotated Outline							ER
G.4	Review for compliance with Win Strategy and Capture Plan Deliverables		CC			CC	CC	ER
G.5	Write First Edition							ER
G.6	Proposal Team reviews First Edition to identify weaknesses and necessary corrective actions		CC			CC	CC	ER
G.7	Write Second Edition							ER
G.8	Mock SSEB Review (Red Team Review)		CC			CC	CC	ER
G.9	Write Third Edition							ER
G.10	Executive Review	FA	CA			CC	CC	CC

	TASKS	Executive	BUM	PM & KC	Staff	BD Manager	Capture Manager	Proposal Manager
G.11	Copy Edit				PS			ER
G.12	Print or Upload				PS			ER
G.13	Submit				PS			ER
G.14	Obtain written receipt for proposal delivery				PS	CC		ER
H	**Proposal Pending**							
H.1	Phone conversations with Contract Officer every two weeks to monitor selection progress and express FIRM interest in winning					ER		
H.2	Prompt response to request for information or clarifications		CC	CC	PS	ER		CC
H.3	Prompt response to BAFO request	FA	ER	CC	PS	CC		CC
H.4	Coordinate and document Lessons Learned					ER		
H.5	Notification of Selection, Loss or Termination					ER		
H.6	Win Celebration	CC	ER	CC		CC	CC	CC
H.7	Negotiate and sign contract	ER	CC			CC		
I	**Business Development During Contract Execution**							
I.1	Periodic update of individual resumes		CC	CC	PS	ER		
I.2	Periodic update of project Past Performance data		CC	CC	PS	ER		
I.3	FIRM Internal Project Performance Assessment		ER			CC		
I.4	Periodic Client assessment of FIRM Performance		ER	CC		CC		
I.5	Obtain and compile letters of commendation from client		CC	CC	PS	ER		

Self Assessment Review

- Does your firm have a business development framework that is understood by all employees?
- Does your firm have a standard approach to responsibility assignment for all business development tasks and activities?
- Does your firm's business development framework rigorously align with its strategic objectives?
- If your firm doesn't have a business development framework, would it help to put one together?
- If your firm doesn't have one, what's stopping you from initiating such a framework?
- Can you name the people in your firm who would support such an effort?
- Would a business development responsibility matrix be a good idea?
- Can you name the people in your firm who would support a responsibility matrix?

FINANCIAL ASPECTS

FIRM's leadership understood early on that revenue growth demanded an influx of new employees, as well as company-wide clarity about the business development framework and financial elements of government contracting. They used the company newsletter, all-hands performance briefings, fireside chats (CEO regularly scheduled meeting with small groups of employees), and any other educational opportunity. The topics they covered:

- Financial and Business Development Elements and Definitions
- Revenue Growth Planning
- Price Proposals

Business development and financial management intersect at pricing of proposals. Pricing must serve the economic health of the firm and be rigorous enough to comply with the government's requirements, practices, and willingness to pay for solutions. Those responsible for financial and business development management must share with colleagues a deep understanding of the issues and challenges of creating and submitting a price proposal.

The single most important factor in FIRM's financial management was selection of the CPA. The owners chose one who had retired from DCAA and now had his own CPA firm. He created the chart of accounts and accounting system, using his intimate knowledge of Cost Accounting Standards (CAS) to explain government contracting practices, Federal Acquisition Regulations on costs and pricing, and requirements and audit practices of the DCAA.

A chart of accounts is the list of all the accounts in a firm's accounting systems. There are small but very important differences between the chart of accounts for commercial business and the chart of accounts for government business. FIRM's chart of accounts meets the financial management needs of both its government contracting and its commercial business. It also facilitates operation of separate profit centers or divisions, enabling independent pricing approaches (different fringe and overhead costs) so that each profit center can tailor pricing to its market and client expectations.

Using its annual revenue growth plan, FIRM sets provisional

Key Topics
- Financial and Business Development Elements and Definitions
- Revenue Growth Planning
- Price Proposals
- Self Assessment Review

Financial and Business Development Elements and Definitions

Certified Public Account

Chart of Accounts

Performance Monitoring

39

percentage rates for fringe, overhead, and general and administration costs (G&A) for government business. These provisional rates are used to develop prices for proposals. While many government contracts do allow FIRM to adjust previously paid invoices to align with actual rates after the end of the fiscal year, FIRM views that as undesirable because it creates budget management and control problems for its clients' program managers. So FIRM manages business operations to match the annual provisional rates by tracking the rates monthly and making operational adjustments during the year to bring costs in line with the provisional figures. FIRM managers also use monthly tracking of planned and actual factors for personnel, contract performance, business development, utilization rate, performance improvement investment, facilities, equipment, and furnishings.

Business Development Costs

FIRM's chart of accounts lists spending in the current year for promotion and marketing (P&M) and for bids and proposals (B&P). Costs for both are estimated monthly, with P&M including conferences and trade shows, revisions to the website, company brochures, press releases, market research, and similar costs not associated with any new contract opportunity. B&P includes positioning activities, capture planning, implementation, creation and production of proposals and/or bids and contract negotiation.

Contract Performance Costs

The chart of accounts and the accounting system allow planning and tracking Direct Costs for each contract, base and option periods, work orders, and work breakdown structure such as phases, tasks, and activities. That way, FIRM can handle projects requiring integrated master plans and submit earned value progress reporting to clients.

Direct Labor Costs

The wages for FIRM's employees billable to contracts (Direct Labor) are used to submit price proposals and bids and to track the cost status of each contract. Direct labor costs do not include wages paid for overhead or G&A labor (indirect labor). They are also used to track business performance factors such as utilization rate, which is the ratio of direct labor costs to direct labor and indirect labor costs combined.

Fringe

Paid time off (vacation, holiday, sick, etc.); medical, health, and dental insurance; retirement and/or pension funding; and other benefits.

Overhead

This takes account of other wages, including incentive compensation, and expenses such as rent related to active contracts.

G&A

This refers to the Indirect Costs such as wages, including incentive compensation, and expenses such as rent that support management and direction of the enterprise.

Fee

This is a pricing element, sometimes mistakenly referred to as profit, that provides funds for FIRM's taxes, interest payments, unallowable costs (non-reimbursable by the government), and net profit. When pricing a proposal, the fee is a percentage of the subtotal of all the contract's costs. The fee is added to the cost subtotal to calculate total contract price. The government uses "weighted guidelines" to determine a fair fee for each contract. FIRM's target contract fee averages eight percent, which it intends to produce a net profit of at least four percent.

Other Direct Costs

Other Direct costs are those required to address contracted scopes of work, including payment to subcontractors as well as vendors, travel and lodging, printing, and similar costs.

Direct Material Cost

This is the cost of materials needed to produce products as contract-required deliverables.

Pricing

For most government contracts, the proposal must state a price and present price backup that includes direct labor costs, fringe, overhead, G&A, other direct costs, material direct costs, and fees for each contract line item.

Incentive Compensation

This is a cost of doing business and not profit sharing and should be included in the chart of accounts as both overhead and G&A compensation. Incentive plans must be documented to be allowable and are subject to a reasonableness test by DCAA.

Profit Sharing

The fee of eight percent, FIRM's target average, provides funds for four elements:

- Disallowable -- expenses not allowed as direct, fringe, overhead, or G&A costs such as alcoholic beverages and political donations.
- Interest paid on borrowed funds.
- Taxes, state and federal.
- Net profit -- FIRM expects profits to average at least four percent of costs, and retains all net profit to minimize borrowing or make new investments. Net profit may also be distributed to owners as a dividend or profit sharing.

Commercial vs Government

A chart of accounts and accounting system set up for a government contracting business will work quite well for a commercial business. But the reverse doesn't work that way. A system designed for commercial business is likely to create significant problems for a government contracting business. Elements such as incentive compensation, profit sharing, independent research and development, marketing and have significant bad debt or other liability costs in the commercial sector. Finally, businesses often anticipate higher net profit for commercial work.

Payment	The government pays invoices in full within 30 days after receiving an approved invoice. FIRM stays on top of invoice approvals and has an internal process to dovetail with that of the government. By the way, a rapid payment procedure is available for small businesses.

Payment

The government pays invoices in full within 30 days after receiving an approved invoice. FIRM stays on top of invoice approvals and has an internal process to dovetail with that of the government. By the way, a rapid payment procedure is available for small businesses.

IR&D

The costs FIRM incurs for Independent Research and Development may be included in overhead and/or G&A if R&D is of potential interest to its government clients. However, on Jan. 30, 2012, the Department of Defense issued new rules in the Defense Federal Acquisition Regulation Supplement ("DFARS") 231.205-18(c). It was finalized, with changes. See 77 Fed. Reg. 4632 (Jan. 30, 2012). For additional information see www.governmentcontractslawblog.com/2012/03/articles/ird/final-rule-for-ird-reports-fails-to-address-most-serious-questions/#

Audit and DCAA

DCAA performs all necessary contract audits for the DoD and other Federal agencies as appropriate and provides accounting and financial advisory services regarding contracts and subcontracts to Components responsible for procurement and contract administration. These services are provided in connection with negotiation, administration, and settlement of contracts and subcontracts. The DCAA performs all annual and contract audits for the Department of Defense and other federal agencies. It also offers accounting and financial advice on contracts and subcontracts to all DoD components that handle procurement and contract administration. Those services come under DCAA's mission to negotiate, administer, and settle contracts and subcontracts to ensure that taxpayer dollars are spent on fair and reasonable contract prices.

Revenue Growth Planning

FIRM began preparing and following an annual revenue growth plan (ARGP). Previously, it had produced an annual business plan requiring detailed input from each cost center. But the plans were long on wish lists and short on producing funds. At that point FIRM had not yet established profit centers, but did have cost centers responsible for various business segments. The problem was that the annual plans had enough ambitious lists for new purchases to exhaust the budget several times over.

By contrast, the ARGP uses a standard approach with a template and adapts the chart of accounts to produce needed financial information. Described below are the eight sections of FIRM's ARGP:

1. Current Year's Revenue - CYR
2. Next Year's Revenue Growth Target - RGT
3. Next Year's Existing Contract Revenue - ECR
4. Next Year's New Contract Revenue - NCR
5. Current New Contract Win Rate

6. Next Year's Proposal Contract Value - PCV
7. Assessment of Current Business Development Pipeline
8. Next Year's Sales Plan and Budget

This section breaks down actual revenue for the prior 11 months and estimated revenue for the last month of the fiscal year. The breakdown includes gross revenue, net revenue (gross revenue minus pass-throughs, such as subcontractor costs), professional service revenue, and product and contract revenue. Each segment is organized by client agency, contract, and FIRM cost center or department.

Burn Rate
At the end of 12 months, 20% of a five year contract has been expended. If 25% of the contract maximum value has been earned, the Burn Rate is 1.25 (25% divided by 20%). However, if only 15% of the maximum value has been earned, the Burn Rate is .75 (15% divided by 20%) A Burn Rate higher than one means money is being earned faster than time is being expended

It also analyzes where 80 percent of the revenue comes from and calculates the contract-by-contract "burn rate," which compares the rate at which the contract maximum value is being used compared to the rate that the contract period of performance is being expended. A burn rate of ONE means the period of performance and maximum value of the contract are being consumed at the same pace. FIRM calculates the contract portfolio, all of FIRM's active contracts, and burn rate for the current year, and uses the forecast burn rate in Section Six (see below) to help determine the total proposal value for next year.

FIRM also uses this section to describe individual contributions to meeting strategic objectives during the current year. The owners consider it vital to recognize such employees, as an ARGP summary is distributed to all employees. The goal is to continue building a culture for consistent long-term revenue growth.

Section Two
Next Year's Revenue Growth Target *(RGT)*

The strategic view of revenue and business development over the past five years, and the five-year forecast for FIRM's government markets, provide the basis for an initial revenue growth target. A breakdown of the RGT by cost center is also included. FIRM's intent for this initial target is aggressive, but not "blue sky."

Section Three
Next Year's Revenue from Existing Contracts *(ECR)*

Analyzing FIRM's portfolio of contracts that will carry over from the current year produces the forecast of next year's revenue from existing contracts. The analysis takes in factors such as the maximum and remaining value of each contract, contract-funding predictions, the historic burn rate of time and money, the client's assessment of performance to date, and the business relationship with the client. Depending on specifics of the current year, future revenue may be divided into categories reflecting the level of reliability, with strategic and tactical recommendations for improving revenue in the riskier levels or categories.

Section Four
Next year's New Contract Revenue *(RGT - ECR =NCR)*

The simple subtraction of REC from next year's RGT produces the amount of revenue that FIRM must obtain from new contracts -- the initial NCR. In some years, it's a single amount, while in other years it's a range of amounts based on the reliability of the NCR.

Section Five
Current New Contract Win Rate

FIRM tracks its win rate on a rolling 24-month basis, calculating both the value and the number of contracts won compared to the proposals submitted. That time span reflects the government's drawn-out procurement process and buying cycle. The CFO had determined that a win rate of 60 percent would produce enough money to invest in business development and support revenue growth of 30 percent to 40 percent, depending on the value of the contracts won and whether the government would fund those contracts to the maximum value.

Section Six
Next Year's Proposal Contract Value
(PCV=5 x RNC)

Comparing the actual win rate for the past 24 months to the 60 percent target win rate formed the basis of forecasting the win rate used to analyze the RNC. Since FIRM's strategy focused on five-year contracts, the RNC must be multiplied by five to determine the PCV for the next year. But the PCV must also be increased to account for the forecast win rate and the forecast burn rate of the new contracts. Finally, FIRM uses the anticipated timing of new procurements to refine the PCV, accounting for the revenue each new contract is likely to produce within the year. To illustrate, contracts won in January would be likely to produce more revenue than contracts won in December.

Section Seven
Assessment of Current Business Development Pipeline

FIRM creates and maintains a four-year pipeline of future contract opportunities using a government business opportunity database augmented by its own market research. It includes both solicitations and contract awards identified for the next year, plus proposals submitted and proposals in process. It compares the maximum value and number of new contract opportunities to the PCV calculated in Section Six. If the value of new contract opportunities exceeds the PCV -- and there are enough new contract opportunities to validate the forecast win rate -- the revenue target becomes a strategic objective. If all FIRM's new contract opportunities fall below the PCV, it adjusts the initial revenue target downward and revises Sections Three through Six. On the other hand, if all new contract opportunities are higher than the PCV, FIRM has to consider raising the initial revenue target and then revising, if necessary, Sections Three through Six

Section Eight
Next Year's Sales Plan and Budget

The final two pieces of information required from FIRM's chart of accounts are amounts spent in the current year for promotion and marketing (P&M) and bids and proposals (B&P). Managers compare that amount to current year net revenue and use the percentages to calculate potential cost (money cannot be spent until the revenue is earned) of next year's P&M and B&P. Those two costs are estimated by month, with P&M including conferences and trade shows, revisions to the website, company brochures, press releases, market research, and similar costs not associated with a new contract opportunity. B&P includes positioning activities, capture planning and implementation, and creation and production

Figure 4.1 Typical FIRM CLIN Price Presentation format

CLIN Number						
CLIN Name						
Number						
1	Direct Labor		Rate	Unit	Quantity	Cost
1.1		Labor Category One				
1.2		Labor Category Two				
1.3		Labor Category Three				
1.4		Labor Category Four				
1.5		Labor Category Five				
1.6		Labor Category Six				
1.7	Total Direct Labor Cost					
			Percent			
2	Direct Labor Fringe		%			
3	Total Direct Labor and Fringe					
4	Overhead		%			
5	Total Direct Labor, Fringe & Overhead					
6	G&A		%			
7	Total Direct Labor, Fringe, Overhead & G&A					
8	Other Direct costs		Description			
8.1		Item One				
8.2		Item Two				
8.3		Item Three				
8.4		Item Four				
8.5		Item Five				
8.6		Item Six				
8.7	Total Other Direct Cost					
9	Subcontractor Costs					
9.1		Subcontractor One				
9.2		Subcontractor Two				
9.3		Subcontractor Three				
9.4	Total Subcontractor Cost					
10	Materials		Description			
10.1		Item One				
10.2		Item Two				
10.3		Item Three				
!0.4	Totl Materials Cost					
11	Total Cost					
12	Fee	%				
13	Price					

of proposals and/or bids.

Pricing

Each proposal to the government must include a price proposal. See Figure 4.1. In most RFPs, contract line item numbers (CLIN) provide detailed requirements. It is not unusual for a RFP to require individual prices for 80 or more CLINs. The price proposal has two major subsections:

- CLIN Prices
- Price Narrative

FIRM researched price narrative via the Internet and discussions with retired government contract officers. It determined that the narrative portion of the price proposal is crucial to its win strategy. Once FIRM grasped the government's process for analyzing price it created a template or guide for a price narrative, which explains the basis for every cost in the price proposal and how FIRM sets the proposed fee percentage and its application to the costs. The primary source of information for preparing price proposals came from these DCAA publications that are available on the DCAA website (see Chapter 6):

- Criteria for Adequate Contract Pricing Proposals
- Adequacy Checklist for Forward Pricing Rate Proposals
- Incurred Cost Adequacy Checklist
- Incurred Cost Electronically
- Information for Contractors
- Preaward Survey of Prospective Contractor Accounting System Checklist

Self Assessment Review

- How could your company create and implement a program to broaden and deepen evey employee's understanding of the financial aspects of your business?
- Does your company have a process or template for annual planning of revenue growth?
- What do you think would be the three most important benefits for your company if there was revenue growth planning process or template?
- Does your company have a standard text or template for the pricing narrative of your price proposals?
- Does that text or template address and satisfy all of the DCAA requirements for pricing?

BUSINESS DEVELOPMENT MANAGEMENT

Muniman came into the Friday partners meeting clearly irritated. Before the agenda could even be presented, he blurted out, "I've spent the entire week meeting with bankers to get that increase in our line of credit for next year, and I've been told in the strongest of terms that this will be the last time if we can't do a lot better when it comes to our revenue forecast accuracy. They don't mind a plus or minus five percent, but we've never gotten closer than 20 percent of the actual amount, and sometimes we're off by 50 percent. With all this revenue growth effort we put out, how can we improve our revenue forecasts?"

The answer lies in business development management. Simply put: A consistent, but improving and disciplined business development process produces a relatively consistent win rate of competitive procurements -- measured in number of proposals and revenue value of proposals.

- The number and value of proposals planned for the coming year, multiplied by the demonstrated win rate, yields the potential revenue from new contracts.
- That potential new contract revenue can be modified by factors such as anticipated award date, amount of pass-throughs such as subcontractors and other direct costs, and other factors needed to define a new contract revenue stream.
- Finally, new contract revenue can be added to the revenue forecast of existing contracts that carry over to the new year to produce a revenue forecast with plus-or-minus five percent accuracy.

That's what FIRM does and it works. To win government contracts and get consistent, long-term revenue growth, FIRM focuses on six steps:

- Building a business development organization.
- Positioning and capture planning.
- Training business development personnel.
- Motivating business development performance.
- Creating effective marketing and sales plans.
- Teaming to win.

Key Topics
- Building a business development organization.
- Positioning and capture planning.
- Training business development personnel.
- Motivating business development performance.
- Creating effective marketing and sales plans.
- Teaming to win.
- Structure of business development investment decisions.
- Operations tracking and monitoring.

A. Building a business development organization
Teamwork: Build a new culture

Think what it takes to build a professional sports team. Simply gathering exceptional talent does not produce memorable performance. Winning requires leadership, a clear vision, a transparent structure, and a shared desire to perform at a high level. And of course, practice is essential.

High rates of growth and winning large contracts demand teamwork -- far more than you'll find in many companies. The team must acknowledge everyone who has a stake in the outcome -- especially for companies with well-defined departments or regions in the company that believe they "own" market turf.

Leadership/shared desire/structure

That requires strong leaders, but it's extremely rare that a single "rainmaker" can win a contract on a "lone wolf" hunting expedition. Real, inclusive teamwork coordinates:

- Customers -- Knowledge of specific markets.
- Technology -- Knowledge of services or products being offered.
- Shared desire -- A motivated team.
- Structure -- Understanding a disciplined process and technique for winning.

Many firms have the first two -- customers and technology -- well in hand. The missing or weakest links are shared desire and structure. So harnessing existing abilities (customers and technologies) with new capabilities (shared desire and structure) is FIRM's key to winning.

To link customers and technologies to new capabilities, management should align business development systems with recognition and incentive systems – all under the high-profile aegis of corporate leadership.

Leadership -- visible senior management

FIRM has demonstrated that business development thrives when strong leaders are overtly involved and willing to share, explain, encourage, and instruct their teams on common approaches and objectives. At a minimum, business unit leaders should initiate and monitor efforts to win large contracts. The groups should meet frequently, by phone and in-person, to review opportunities. At the same time, senior corporate management should be involved in or at least fully aware of any developments.

Shared desire to team

Even firms with a business development structure often rely on the "star salesman" or "rainmaker" to bring in the big programs. But FIRM has realized that fails to recognize the importance of embracing everyone so that the group sees itself as a team and not just a conglomeration of staff supporting the "big guy" who gets all the credit.

Winning contracts, especially large contracts, counts on diverse skills -- marketing, business analysis, finance, program management, technology and/or services delivery, warranties, proposal management, and proposal writing. Specialists in each field must understand their roles in winning the contract and strive to be part of the success. Rainmakers might get the prospective client interested, but it takes a motivated organization to respond to a client's needs and win the contract.

You have a better chance of winning if you 1) focus existing company talents, 2) use consultants, and 3) are poised to rapidly produce high-quality proposals and business development materials.

We must compete in a world where superb color graphics and proposal writer training are commonplace. Indeed, many companies find that their spiffiest proposal barely keeps up with the competition. So try to create a new staff capability that pays for itself with increased revenue from new contracts.

Consider creating a "proposal shop"

Many companies, even long-time government contractors, lack a well-defined structure attuned to the business development cycle and prepared to provide a common language while institutionalizing routine and constantly examining opportunities.

High-growth companies use formal systems to evaluate and track new business opportunities. Inevitably, they yield two benefits: dependable revenue forecasts and steadily improving business development.

Structure: business development systems, the key to continuous improvement

The key: Those systems evaluate every new business opportunity for investment potential. They reduce or eliminate investments that will not bear fruit and focus on potential winners, all the while carefully tracking what it takes to get there. That way, the organization knows what works and what doesn't work. There is no clearer path to future success.

Capture, or positioning, planning is crucial to winning large contracts. But it must be a mandatory, formal process scrutinized at the top. Prepared by a capture team, FIRM's plans are reviewed by high-level management and various "experts." Once approved, they form the baseline for monitoring all actions aimed at winning.

B. Capture Planning

The real goal of the capture plan is to win before the RFP is issued or before the firm is invited to present. A good capture plan moves the client to the position where working with your firm is believed to be the best option.

Don't expect much from business development training in formal classroom or seminar settings. What produces the best revenue growth is modified on-the-job training (MOJT). MOJT combines real-life daily practice with delivery of relevant material tied to a company's BD system.

C. Business Development (BD) Training

MOJT works with new business opportunities, solving real problems and accomplishing much. What's more, it trains the trainers -- creating a cadre of leaders who spread the knowledge through your organization. That way, excellence is contagious. Now don't take that to mean that you should shun the occasional seminar. Integrated into an aggressive MOJT program, classroom training can help drive performance.

D. Motivating Business Development Performance

Recognition -- Celebrate victory! Your company is so much more than technology and structure. It's all about people, hard-working people who deserve credit for a job well done. Every big contract win should spark a victory celebration led by senior management heaping praise on the winning team. That means the ENTIRE TEAM – not just key sales professionals and their top lieutenants. And think about publishing an internal newsletter to announce successes and acknowledge the teams in detail. Recognition is crucial to building and sustaining a winning culture.

In case we weren't clear: Celebrate victory!

Incentive -- The team is the target: Incentive compensation for large contract business development must recognize teamwork. Bonuses based on individual performance often end up disappointing those who are not recognized, which is no way to build cohesion. ClientView has developed five principles for integrated incentive plans that work:

- **Motivation** – To drive performance to higher levels employ a full slate of all the motivational factors that affect human behavior – power, wealth, respect, affection, skill, rectitude, well-being, and enlightenment.
- **Transparency** – How you decide who gets incentives and the amount or nature of the incentive is straightforward and well understood by employees.
- **Parity** – Employees have confidence in the fairness of your incentive system.
- **Team award** – Recognize all contributors to the winning effort.
- **Apportionment** – The amount or nature of the incentive reflects the value of the individual's contribution to the winning effort.

Winning large contracts requires alignment of behavior, systems, recognition, and reward. That makes integrated incentive compensation well worth the effort.

E. Effective Marketing and Sales Efforts

Identifying and implementing the things required to win while also identifying and avoiding things that can cause you to lose is one way to define effective marketing and sales efforts. FIRM has found that the best method for identifying both is to listening; also known as strategic interviewing. Strategic interviewing is crucial to understanding the prospective client. Many companies we survey wrongly believe that business development success depends on sales calls that present their strengths to a potential client in compelling fashion.

But there's much more to it. Untimely or awkward presentation of company capabilities is a common marketing and sales mistake. If you make a compelling presentation at a time when your prospective client has no interest in selecting a company, you will have wasted not only your time, but also the time of your prospective client. A general rule to use is that before the RFP is released focus your sales efforts on understanding the mission, challenges, and obstacles confronting your prospective client. This is the understanding that builds an appreciation for what is required to win and what must be avoided to prevent losing,

The surest path to successful marketing and sales is LISTENING. Train your employees to listen effectively and assertively, asking questions based on what they hear, not just waiting to make their pitch. They should learn to make sales calls without brochures, slides, pamphlets, and books. All they need are business cards and a note pad.

Careful listening, also known as strategic interviewing, is the only way to respond precisely and directly to your client's needs. It works better than any other technique for repeat business and new business.

In fact, FIRM listens first and then presents their capabilities when the prospect shows some interest. That way FIRM tailors the pitch to meet customer's specific needs and challenges. FIRM never, ever, presents corporate capabilities as a way to introduce FIRM. The company's one sentence "elevator speech" is more than sufficient. Again, listen to the customer first.

Compliance is the key to avoid losing. In competitive procurements you should pay as much attention to not losing as you do to winning. That is, do not give proposal reviewers a reason to disqualify you. To avoid losing, you should: Read every request for proposal or information with extreme care; listen in detail to your prospective customers' comments; understand their needs and the nature of their decision-making; and be absolutely sure that you address every nuance fully in your response. Failure to respond to some minute detail can lead to a rejected proposal.

Rarely are selection committees of one mind. Some members may favor your selection, but others see it in a different light, with a minor oversight in a presentation or proposal giving them all the evidence they need to vote you down. Your failure to be totally compliant and fully responsive can be the rope that hangs you.

F. Teaming to Win

Whether you're selecting subcontractors for your team or presenting your company as a potential member of a prime contractor's team, the issues to be addressed are the same:

- Is the subcontractor fully capable of performing assigned work in complete compliance with contract requirements, within budget, on time, and at the required quality level?
- Does the subcontractor bring assets to the prime's team that clearly increase the chances of winning the contract?

Mechanics of Winning

Business Development Funnel --Track business development performance in six process phases:

- Lead -- No decision.

- Opportunity – Investment decision that a lead meets FIRM's criteria for additional development.

- Target – Investment decision that FIRM has a reasonable win strategy supported by credible information and a B&P number.

- Proposal in process – Investment decision that FIRM should prepare a proposal.

- Proposal pending – Investment decision to submit proposal, respond to various contracting officer requests, and await a decision by the government.

This is the "Big Picture" for the test in Chapter 4.

- Win, lose, or terminated -- Self-explanatory

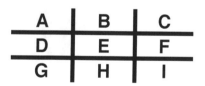

If you have this "Big Picture" in mind it is easy to remember which symbol goes with each letter.

Win Rate - FIRM measures business development performance over a rolling 24-month period to reflect the long government procurement process. They measure both the potential maximum value of new contracts and the number of leads, opportunities, targets, proposals in process, proposals pending, and win/lose/terminated each month.

For consistency and to ensure value of data FIRM always uses the total maximum amount the government will have to pay over the life of the contract, including all costs of the prime contract, subcontractors, expenses, materials, and supplies.

Incentive Compensation and Recognition - Include all employees in a comprehensive business development incentive program. Define levels of responsibility and contribution to reach strategic objectives. Employ a full slate of all the motivational factors that affect human behavior – power, wealth, respect, affection, skill, rectitude, well-being, and enlightenment. Do not include profit sharing.

Qualification Process and Forms - Integrated into the process are four decision points or filters that help FIRM focus on the most promising opportunities. Each one requires CEO approval of business development investment before proceeding. They are:

1. Lead to Opportunity -- This helps FIRM decide if a lead is truly an opportunity. It looks into whether the lead is real (real client, real need, and real money) and if it fits FIRM (core competencies, strategic fit, and corporate risk). A lead that passes through this filter is called a "QUALIFIED OPPORTUNITY."

2. Opportunity to Target -- The second filter promotes a QUALIFIED OPPORTUNITY to a TARGET. It requires an acceptable win strategy based on information obtained directly from the prospect. For high-priority opportunities, a formal capture plan may be the best option.

3. Target to Proposal In Process-- The third filter promotes a TARGET to a PROPOSAL IN PROCESS. It's the GO/NOGO decision for FIRM's biggest investment.

4. Proposal In Process to Proposal Pending - The final filter is the decision to submit the proposal; promoting it from Proposal In Process to Proposal Pending and authorizes additional investments for responses to interrogatories, best and final offers and contract negotiation. The four filter forms are presented below and integrated into the FIRM business development management system.

A simplified version of these steps is used to track and evaluate task order opportunities in IDIQ contracts

Investment Decision Filters

Figure 5.1 - Filter One - LEAD to OPPORTUNITY

Category	Required Informtion
Prospect	Contract or Solicitation Name and number
	Agency Name
	Department Name
	Office Name
	Program Name
Value	Government Estimate
	Interpretation of Government's Level of Effort
	Other
Objectives	Government's Objectives
	Expected Period of Performance
	Expected RFP Issue Date
	Expected Cotract Award Date
FIRM Fit	Percent of Contract Expected to be within FIRM's core compentencies
	Percent of Contract Expected to Align with FIRM's Strategic Plan/Objectives
	FIT Analysis - see example

Look for leads that have good potential for growth, rather than just an initial large revenue haul. Prime contracts are a plus because companies that are usually subs can be construed as unable to do big projects, and may be viewed unfavorably by larger programs.

Example of FIT analysis (guidance only – not required)
FIRM's guide for FIT analysis is presented in Figure 5.2 below.
Figure 5.2 Strategic Fit Analysis Guide

Characteristic	Typical Reasons
This would be a FIRM prime contract	1. Control – staffing, responsibility, share of work & clearances, quality control 2. Visibility & ability to meet with customer 3. More profitable 4. Better able to infuse FIRM identity in new employees 5. Higher up in "food chain" – viewed as more capable by customers, which leads to more success on future proposals.
This fits FIRM's core competencies	1. This is the area FIRM does well in (as opposed to being a boutique with one or two specialties) 2. We have the past performance to help with the win.
This is a contract with an organization that is a previous FIRM client	1. It is likely to narrow the competition or give us an advantage 2. It allows us to use some good past performance citations that we might not otherwise be able to use. 3. It gives us a contract where we can hire new people and expand our capabilities.
The contract has some positions we can fill with new hires	1. Build staff to work on FIRM contracts. 2. Allows us to offer the career incentive for good people to come to FIRM.
The contract is in an area in which there is potential growth – either with the same client or with other clients needing similar work	1. Make future growth easier and cheaper to pursue 2. Become known for a new area of expertise
The contract requires many of the same skills FIRM has, but also a few that they do not have	1. Opportunity to gradually (with lower risk) expand our capabilities. 2. Offers our existing people potential for career advancement
We can make a good profit on the contract.	1. We need a profit to keep corporation going 2. Profit can help achieve other goals, such as training.

Figure 5.3 Filter Two – OPPORTUNITY to TARGET

#	Capture Plan Component	Full Plan	Mini Plan
Business Unit Manager and CEO determine if a FULL or MINI capture plan is required			
1	Name of Program	X	X
2	Name of Capture Manager	X	X
3	Members of Capture Team		
4	Name of Procurement Authority	X	X
5	Description of issues at stake	X	X
6	Type of contract anticipated	X	X
7	Estimated Maximum contract value	X	X
8	Estimated Period of Performance	X	X
9	Anticipated date RFP will be released	X	X
10	Anticipated date proposal due	X	X

#	Capture Plan Component	Full Plan	Mini Plan
	Business Unit Manager and CEO determine if a FULL or MINI capture plan is required		
11	Anticipated date that contract will be awarded	X	X
12	Expected Evaluation Factors	X	X
13	People in prospect's organization who are candidates for the Source Selection Evaluation Board, current position and phone number, potential role in selection process	X	
14	History of events in the program this contract will support	X	
15	Significant competitors with size classification, prime or sub role, strengths and weaknesses	X	
16	Table comparing significant competitors with expected Evaluation Factors	X	
17	Table comparing significant competitors with Statement of Work elements or factors	X	
18	Strength and weakness analysis of competitive teams (Prime with subs)	X	
19	Price to win analysis including Government estimate, Prevailing labor rates for client and local, competitor's pricing data and strategies, expected proposal instructions and evaluation factors, plan for corporate review, and cost to perform estimate	X	
20	Proposal Team positions and responsible person	X	
21	Teaming specifications considering prospect's Statement of Objectives, Statement of Work, and Capability Requirements with FIRM Gap Analysis	X	
22	Corporate risks and mitigation analysis	X	X
23	FIRM internal Teams – Proposal and Performing	X	X
24	FIRM External Team – Name of firm, Contribution to winning, and contribution to performing	X	X
25	Prospect concerns and FIRM discriminators	X	X
26	Win strategy	X	X
27	Win strategy initiatives directed toward prospect	X	X
28	Win Strategy initiatives directed toward FIRM employees	X	
29	Win strategy initiatives directed toward the proposal	X	
30	Action Plan – Visits to key prospect personnel (What, Who, and When)	X	
31	Action Plan – Competition Assessment (What, Who, and When)		
32	Action Plan – Teaming (What, Who, and When)	X	
33	Action Plan - Marketing and Proposal Information (What, Who, and When)	X	
34	Action Plan – Proposal Creation and Production (What, Who, and When)	X	
35	Action Plan – FIRM's image and reputation (What, Who, and When)	X	
36	Action Plan – Influencing the Procurement (What, Who, and When)	X	
37	Results of Capture Plan Review	X	X

Figure 5.4   Business Development Investment Decision Matrix (Repeated from Chapter 3)

Win Probability Assessment For Approval of Funds to Prepare Proposal

SCORE OF 80 OUT OF 100 REQUIRED FOR APPROVAL TO PREPARE PROPOSAL

#	Criteria	ALL COMPETITORS ARE LIKELY TO BE BETTER THAN US		WE ARE BETTER THAN SOME COMPETITORS		WE ARE BETTER THAN MOST COMPETITORS			WE ARE EQUAL TO THE STRONGEST COMPETITOR	WE ARE BETTER THAN THE STRONGEST COMPETITOR IN SOME ASPECTS	WE ARE BETTER THAN ALL COMPETITORS - INMATCHED
		1	2	3	4	5	6	7	8	9	10
1	Do we understand the prospect's challenge and have a concise plan for helping the project be successful?										
2	Does the prospect know us as a leading firm in the issues of this SOW?										
3	Does the prospect know our Project Manager and key staff as outstanding professionals?										
4	Do we and our team members have all of the capabilities required to perform successfully?										
5	Does this contract fit our strategic plan and provide strategic advantages?										
6	Can we prepare an exceptional winning proposal?										
7	Can we submit a competitive price?										
8	Can we manage or mitigate all risks of this contract?										
9	Are our Past Performance Assessments relevant and exceptional?										
10	Do we know the competition and have a plan to beat them?										
Total Score											

Tracking business opportunities demands rigorous research into investment opportunities. You can get that from sales calls, public information on the Internet, and database services that are available for a fee. Be particularly alert for information from employees who work with existing clients. It's not unusual for government managers and technical personnel to pass along tidbits about future procurements. Whatever the source, you must process that intelligence to develop a strategy for winning a future contract and growing your revenue.

Sales calls -- You're making the visit because you need critical information to help understand your prospective client's mission, challenges, and obstacles. It is only through this understanding that you can identify and define critical performance discriminators that must be presented in the winning proposal.

FIRM always plans as sales call by:
*   Clearly defining the objective of the sales call (What they want to come away with)
*   Who will make the sales call considering position in FIRM, education and career background, gender and other factors compared to who will be participating from the prospective client's organization
*   How the information will be recorded during the meeting
*   Potential follow-up actions that might be offered at the conclusion of the meeting - typically some additional relevant information the FIRM could provide at a future meeting

Public information -- Websites searches on FedBizOps, ProcNet, or other government websites are abundant information sources on near-term procurements.

Database services -- Commercial services collect and organize information on government procurements for a fee or subscription payment. What they offer can be downloaded to a spreadsheet to help you understand the full spectrum of past and present procurements as well as plans for procurements over the next five to ten years. Look also for an abundance of information, such as the maximum value of a future contract, the contact information of the contract officer, the purpose of the contract, and other information relevant to the development of your win strategy.

Below in Figure 5.5 is the information typically collected and compiled by FIRM for each step in the business development funnel. FIRM collects this information and compiles it in spreadsheets that are updated during meetings of the FIRM Business Development Council.

Business Development Tracking and Monitoring

Some of the private sector Government Business Development Database services that may be found in a Google search:

*   govdirections.com
*   bidnet.com
*   usgovinfo.about.com/ od/moneymatters/a/ ctopportunities.htm
*   fedmine.us/fedmine/ Home.html
*   governmentbids.com
*   businessopportunity. com/government-opportunities/
*   govwin.com
*   epipeline.com/

Figure 5.5 Data required for tracking and managing business development

LEAD

BD Number	Assign a tracking number to every LEAD entered into your BD tracking system. This number will stay with the opportunity through all steps in the business development funnel.
Number -- Current LEAD quantity	Sequentially number current leads so that the total number of current LEADs is available.
Name of procurement	The name being used to identify this procurement
Name of customer or client	Name of the government agency, department, or office responsible for this LEAD
Purpose	Very brief description of the purpose or objective of this procurement
Contract -- price structure	Identify type of contract -- firm fixed price, cost plus fee, or other
Contract -- type	IDIQ (indefinite duration, indefinite quantity), defined scope of work, or other
Contract -- method	Identify procurement method -- full and open, small business set-aside, or other
Contract -- maximum value	Information from government sources indicating the maximum estimated amount the government believes the contract will cost
Time line -- release	Date the RFP is scheduled to be released by the government
Time line – due	Date that proposals are scheduled or expected to be submitted
Time line -- award	Date estimated for the award of contract or notification of selection
Comments	Any other relevant information regarding this procurement

OPPORTUNITY

All LEAD Information	See LEAD above
Contacts – date	Date of meeting with a key contact in the government agency responsible for this procurement
Contacts -- name & position	Name and position of each contact participating in the meeting
Contacts -- phone	Each contact's phone number
Contacts -- address	Each contact's mailing address
Contacts -- email	Each contact's email address
Value -- maximum value	Update maximum value information
Value --net value	Maximum value to the prime minus estimated pass- through for vendors, subcontractors, consultants, and other direct costs
Capture plan Status and date of capture plan	- waived by management, in process, under review, or approved

TARGET

All LEAD information	See LEAD above
All OPPORTUNITY information	See OPPORTUNITY above
Sales calls	Status of sales calls required by capture plan
Competitors	Status of competitor identification and analysis required by capture plan
Team	Status of SOW analysis, identification of teaming requirements, team strategy and objectives, teaming negotiations, and teaming agreements
Positioning deliverables	Status of each positioning deliverable (information, reports, and other data for use in the proposal preparation) required in the capture plan
Proposal plan	Status of management review and approval of the budget and cost for preparation of a proposal

PROPOSAL IN PROCESS

All LEAD information	See LEAD above
All OPPORTUNITY information	See OPPORTUNITY above
All TARGET information	See TARGET above

PROPOSAL PENDING

All LEAD information	See LEAD above
All OPPORTUNITY information	See OPPORTUNITY above
All TARGET information	See TARGET above
Price -- total	Total price submitted for total contract
Price -- total net	Price total minus the pass-through costs for vendors, subcontractors, consultants, and ODCs
Award date	Expected award date
Revenue lag	Estimated period of time between contract award and receipt of payment for first invoice

Proposals Won, Lost, or Terminated

All LEAD information	See LEAD above
All OPPORTUNITY information	See OPPORTUNITY above

Proposals Won, Lost, or Terminated	
All TARGET information	See TARGET above
All PROPOSAL PENDING information	See PROPOSAL PENDING above
Price -- amounts as awarded in contract	Update of PRICE information
Award date	Actual award date
Award status	Won, lost, or terminated

Operations Monitoring to Enhance Revenue Growth

One imperative and nonnegotiable requirement is control of costs. For government contracting, DCAA can audit costs annually, prior to a contract award, during the contract award, or after contract completion. Don't forget that prices submitted in proposals often must be certified for their accuracy. That means that if the price you submit in a contract bid is shown later to be in error, the government can adjust your payment accordingly. That could happen even after the contract has been completed -- meaning you may be forced to return funds.

One cost element of particular concern is the overhead rate, particularly since many contracts are multi-year commitments. It's quite a challenge to state a price that will be current for five years while accommodating overhead projections. For its part, FIRM tracks overhead monthly, and includes other performance parameters (see Figure 5.6) to ensure that cost factors used to set price prove out in actual operations.

The spreadsheet in Figure 5.6 is a simplified example of FIRM's system for tracking planned and actual performance values. It monitors planned or forecast values of several performance factors for each month, and compares them with the actual performance value each month. In addition, it presents the cumulative planned and actual performance values for the year.

Figure 5.6 Example of a fiscal month

SEPTEMBER 2013						
Sunday	**Monday**	**Tuesday**	**Wednesday**	**Thursday**	**Friday**	**Saturday**
1	2	3 Start of fiscal month	4	5	6	7
8	9	10	11	12	13	14
15	16	17	18	19	20	21
22	23	24	25	26	27 End of fiscal month	28 Invoices prepared
29 Invoices Prepared	30 Invoices Submitted	1	2	3	4	5

Figure 5.7 Annual Operations Monitoring of Planned and Actual Performance

Fiscal Time Period	Cumulative for Fiscal Year		Fiscal Month 1 to 12 - Expand to show all months	
Planned & Actual	Planned	Actual	Planned	Actual
Fiscal Work Days				
FINANCIAL PERFORMANCE				
Gross Revenue				
Net Revenue				
Utilization Rate %				
Fringe Rate%				
Overhead % (Off-Site)				
Overhead % (On-Site)				
G&A%				
BUSINESS DEVELOPMENT				
Proposal Win Rate % - Number				
Proposal Win Rate % - Value $				
Proposals Pending - N				
Proposals Pending - V				
PIP - Number				
PIP - Value				
Target - Number				
Target - Value				
Qualified - Number				
Qualified - Value				
PERSONNEL				
Total FTEs				
Total Employees				
Total 1099s				
Total Off-Site Personnel				
Total On-Site Personnel				
Gross Floor are/Off site personnel				
New hires				
Terminations				
CONTRACT PORTFOLIO				
Remaining Max Value				
Remainig Auth Backlog				
Portfolio Burn Rate				

The categories monitored with this system include:

- Financial performance
- Business development
- Personnel
- Contract portfolio.

FIRM prepares a fiscal calendar that maximizes the number of fiscal weeks ending on Fridays and minimizes the number of fiscal months that end in mid-week. It also determines the number of fiscal days in each week and uses it to spread labor-based revenue over the year. FIRM minimizes the time for accounts receivable by working on Saturday and Sunday at the end of each fiscal month to expedite posting of invoices to clients.

The calendar for the month of September 2013 in Figure 5.6 illustrates the fiscal calendar concepts used by FIRM. September's fiscal days have a white background; October's a light grey, and non-fiscal days have a medium grey background. The example shows that FIRM's first day of fiscal September is September 3 and not Monday, which is Labor Day, a holiday, and therefore, not a fiscal day. This means the first week of fiscal September has only 32 work hours while the other four weeks each have 40 work hours. Fiscal September actually ends on September 27 and fiscal October begins on Septmber 30. Note that invoices for the work performed in fiscal September are submitted to the clients electronically on September 30, marking the start of the 30-day payment period required by contract.

Below are the definitions of the items that FIRM monitors each month as shown in Figure 5.7.

Financial Performance

Gross revenue -- since bad debt is a rarity in government contracting, FIRM posts the total amount invoiced each fiscal month as the gross revenue number being monitored.

Net revenue -- FIRM subtracts total pass-through direct revenue from gross revenue to determine the net revenue, with the goal of identifying total funds to operate FIRM.

Utilization rate -- FIRM divides the total cost of direct labor by the total cost of all direct and indirect labor to determine this rate, with a target of 70 percent to 77 percent. It is monitored weekly. Utilization rate serves as early warning that there may be a problem developing in overhead, G&A, and/or net profit.

Fringe rate -- FIRM prorates or spreads the cost of fringe evenly over all fiscal weeks to eliminate wild fluctuations for the actual time when unpaid overtime is incurred. Each month it assesses the prorated amounts to account for any changes to projections for the year and makes needed adjustments.

Overhead (off-site) -- FIRM has two overhead rates. The first, off-site, is for personnel who work at FIRM's facilities. That overhead is higher than the one for personnel who work at the government's facilities.

Overhead (on-site) -- This rate for personnel working at government facilities is lower than for the personnel who work at government's facilities.

FIRM could also create different overhead rates for different profit centers of company divisions and subsidiaries as long as each has a dedicated accounting system.

G&A -- The general and administrative rate covers all non-billable expenses of managing and directing the company.

Business Development (typical categories for all the ones listed here include full and open, small business set-aside, and IDIQ.)

Proposal win rate number percentage -- This is the number of winning proposals in a competitive category divided by the number of all proposals in that category that were submitted.

Proposal win rate value percentage -- This is the total maximum value of proposals in a competitive category that have been won divided by the total maximum value of all proposals in that category submitted.

Proposals pending number (PPN) -- This is the number of proposals in a competitive category that have been submitted and not yet awarded.

Proposals pending value(PPV) -- This is the total value of proposals in a competitive category that have been submitted and not yet awarded.

Proposals in process number (PIPN) -- This is the number of proposals in a competitive category that have been approved by management, but not yet submitted.

Proposals in process value (PIPV) -- This is the total value of proposals in a competitive category that have been approved by management, but not yet submitted.

Target number (TN) - This is the number of opportunities in a competitive category that have capture plans approved by management, but are not yet approved for proposal preparation.

Target value – (TV) - This is the total value of opportunities in a competitive category that have capture plans approved by management, but are not yet approved for proposal preparation.

Business Development

Qualified number -- (QN) - This is the number of LEADs in a competitive category that have enough information for a management go-ahead to develop and implement a capture plan, but do not yet have an approved capture plan.

Qualified value -- (QV) - This is the total value of LEADs in a competitive category that have enough information for a management go-ahead to develop and implement a capture plan, but do not yet have an approved capture plan.

Personnel

Total FTEs -- Total paid labor hours divided by the standard workweek, typically 40 hours.

Total employees -- Total number of full and part-time employees who receive fringe benefits.

Total 1099s and part-time -- Total number of full and part-time personnel who do not receive fringe benefits.

Total off-site personnel -- Total number of full and part-time employees, 1099s, and other part-timers who work in facilities owned or leased by the FIRM.

Total on-site personnel -- Total number of full and part-time employees, 1099s, and other part-timers who work in facilities provided by the government.

Facilities gross floor area per off-site personnel -- Gross floor area of facilities owned or leased by the FIRM that is used to perform work required by active government contracts divided by total off-site personnel.

Contract Portfolio

Remaining value -- Remaining maximum value of active government contracts.

Remaining authorized backlog -- Remaining value of the authorized work or backlog in the active contract portfolio.

Portfolio burn rate – Compares time and money expended on a contract vs. the contract schedule and budget. The tracking sheet compares the percent of performance time for all active contracts with the percent the maximum value of all active contracts has been used. A comparison number of ONE indicates the budget and schedule are being used at the same rate. A comparison number of less than ONE shows that budget is being used up faster than the schedule, and a number greater than ONE indicates the schedule will be exceeded before the budget is used up.

- Can you name three things your firm could do to build a better business development organization?
- What is your company's strongest attribute in business development?
- What is the weakest?
- How can the investment decisions in your company be structured and made more effective?
- Does your company have a well defined operations monitoring system?

ACQUISITION INFORMATION

Information sources and their URLs are listed below for various Government entities that have involvement or are relevant to the acquisition and procurement process.

The FAR Is the primary rule book for all govenrment contracting. It is organized in eight subchapters. Each subchapter contain a number of parts (54 in total) and many subparts. The FAR is readily available on the internet and can be searched by topic, such as "Influencing procurement in FAR." For access to total FAR you may go to:

http://www.acquisition.gov/far/

The DFARS is a supplement to the FAR. It contains the acquisition rules and guidance to facilitate the acquisition workforce as they acquire the goods and services DoD requires to ensure America's warfighters continued worldwide success. It is organized in 52 Parts, each of which contains a number of subparts. The DFARS may be downoaded at:

http://www.acq.osd.mil/dpap/dars/dfarspgi/current/ index.html

The Defense Contract Audit Agency, is under the authority, direction, and control of the Under Secretary of Defense (Comptroller), (USD(C))/Chief Financial Officer (CFO), Department of Defense. The DCAA, while serving the public interest as its primary customer, shall perform all necessary contract audits for the Department of Defense and provide accounting and financial advisory services regarding contracts and subcontracts to all DoD Components responsible for procurement and contract administration. These services are provided in connection with negotiation, administration, and settlement of contracts and subcontracts to ensure taxpayer dollars are spent on fair and reasonable contract prices. The DCAA shall provide contract audit services to other Federal agencies as appropriate.

http://www.dcaa.mil

Key Topics
- Sources of information
- Acquisition Process Scenarios

FAR - Federal Acquisition Regulations

DFARS - Defense Federal Acquisition Regulation Supplement

DCAA - Defense Contract Audit Agency

DCMA - Defense Contract Management Agency

The Defense Contract Management Agency (DCMA) is the Department of Defense (DoD) component that works directly with Defense suppliers to help ensure that DoD, Federal, and allied government supplies and services are delivered on time, at projected cost, and meet all performance requirements. DCMA directly contributes to the military readiness of the United States and its allies, and helps preserve the nation's freedom.

DCMA professionals serve as "information brokers" and in-plant representatives for military, Federal, and allied government buying agencies -- both during the initial stages of the acquisition cycle and throughout the life of the resulting contracts.

Before contract award, DCMA provides advice and information to help construct effective solicitations, identify potential risks, select the most capable contractors, and write contracts that meet the needs of our customers in DoD, Federal and allied government agencies.

After contract award, DCMA monitors contractors' performance and management systems to ensure that cost, product performance, and delivery schedules are in compliance with the terms and conditions of the contracts.

http://www.dcma.mil/about.cfm

SAM - System for Award Mangement

SAM is a Federal Government owned and operated, free web site that consolidates the capabilities in CCR/FedReg, ORCA, and EPLS. Future phases of SAM will add the capabilities of other systems used in Federal procurement and awards processes.

It combines the federal procurement systems and the Catalog of Federal Domestic Assistance into one new system. This consolidation is being done in phases. The first phase of SAM includes the functionality from the following systems:
  • Central Contractor Registry (CCR)
  * Federal Agency Registration (Fedreg)
  * Online Representations and Certifications Application
  * Excluded Parties List System (EPLS).

How will SAM benefit government contractors?The overarching benefits of SAM include streamlined and integrated processes, elimination of data redundancies, and reduced costs while providing improved capability.

All Government contractors are required to be registered on SAM.

https://www.sam.gov

Acquisition.gov is an E-Gov Initiative that aggregates federal acquisition content by providing one website for regulations, systems, resources, opportunities, and training.

This website was designed to create an easily navigable resource to share the efforts to achieve its vision of more efficient and transparent practices through better use of information, people, processes and technology.

EPLS System retirement
The EPLS system will be retired on November 21, 2012. All exclusions capabilities will be found exclusively in SAM (www.sam. gov) beginning November 22, 2012. Please see these Helpful Hints for more information.

www.acquisition.gov

Acquisition.gov

The core mission of Keeping America Informed, dated to 1813 when Congress determined to make information regarding the work of the three branches of Government available to all Americans. The U.S GPO provides publishing and dissemination services for the official and authentic government publications to Congress, Federal agencies, Federal depository libraries, and the American public.

http://www.gpo.gov/

GPO - Government Printing Office

FAPIIS is a web-enabled application that is used to collect contractor and grantee performance information including Terminations for Cause or Default, Defective Cost and Pricing Data, Determinations of Non-Responsibility, Terminations for Material Failure to Comply (grants), Recipient Not Qualified Determinations (grants), DoD Determination of Contractor Fault and Administrative Agreements. Once records are completed in FAPIIS, they become available in the Federal Past Performance Information Retrieval System (PPIRS) where they are used to support future acquisitions.

FAPIIS - Federal Awardees Performance and Integrity Information System

Search FAPIIS Records
Search Instructions:Search by DUNS, CAGE, or by selecting a filter from the dropdown box. NOTE: If you enter multiple search criteria, the DUNS code will take precedence.
CAGE or DUNS/DUNSPLUS4 searches must be exact. CAGE must be 5 characters; DUNS must be either 9 or 13 characters.

Special Search Note: It is possible in the FAPIIS application that a contractor may not have a CAGE CODE. If you search by CAGE and do not get the contractor you are looking for, try again using the 'Name' search option. Note some of the Extended Systems do not require DUNS. If your search of the FAPIIS system does not produce a Performance Information section of SAM record, you can go directly to the System for Award Management (SAM) https://www.sam.gov/ and use the 'Advanced Search' option to locate the entity of interest.

To search for an individual by name, search using the 'Contains' option and specify only the person's last name.

https://www.fapiis.gov

USAspending.gov

The Federal Funding Accountability and Transparency Act (FFATA) of 2006, full text of the Transparency Act , requires that the Office of Management and Budget (OMB) establish a single searchable website, accessible to the public at no cost, which includes for each Federal award:

1. the name of the entity receiving the award;
2. the amount of the award;
3. information on the award including transaction type, funding agency, etc;
4. the location of the entity receiving the award; and
5. a unique identifier of the entity receiving the award.

USAspending.gov was first launched in December 2007 to fulfill these requirements. Prime award information shown on the website is provided by Federal Agencies through four main source systems (see Sources of Data). USAspending.gov receives and displays data pertaining to obligations (amounts awarded for federally sponsored projects during a given budget period), not outlays or expenditures (actual cash disbursements made against each project). Read the latest OMB-issued memoranda M-09-19, "Guidance on Data Submission under the Federal Funding Accountability and Transparency Act" as it provides guidance to agencies on how to report information to USAspending.gov.
USAspending.gov has been recently updated in October 2010 to display of first-tier sub-award data (subcontracts and subgrants). Sub-award information shown on the website is provided by FSRS (see Sources of Data). The latest guidance documents pertaining to sub-award reporting can be found under News.

http://www.usaspending.gov

FBO - Federal Business Opportunities

FBO enables information searches of the more than 26,000 active federal opportunities.

https://www.fbo.gov

Business USA

- Learn about financing options for your business at workshops. Starting and managing a business

- Do you need help with federal contracting? Here's a list of resources to help you: http://t.co/VCkUvEs4 #GovCon

http://business.usa.gov

Advocacy
The voice of small business on Capitol Hill since it was created in 1976, the Office of Advocacy works to protect, strengthen and represent the interests of the nation's small businesses within the Federal Government.

Ombudsman
If excessive fines, penalties, or unfair regulatory enforcement by federal agencies are problems for your small business, you have a voice in Washington, D.C., through SBA's Office of the National Ombudsman.

Inspector General
The Office of the Inspector General conducts audits, investigations and other reviews to deter and detect waste, fraud and abuse in SBA programs and operations and to promote agency efficiency and effectiveness.

SBA Programs
Small business is America's most powerful engine of opportunity and economic growth. That's where SBA comes in. SBA offers a variety of programs and support services to help you navigate the issues you face with your initial applications, and resources to help after you open for business.

www.sba.gov

SBA - Small Business Administration

Providing Value ... from Strategy to Proposals
Our approach is founded on understanding how your clients view and perceive value in your firm. We then convey that understanding to you and, in collaboration with you, work to define how you may adjust your approach to your clients and achieve your strategic objectives. Using this principle, we have helped our clients' firms win more than $25 billion in Government Contracts.

Professional services and technology firms working with government clientele face unique challenges in business development and, therefore, frequently find obstacles inhibiting revenue growth. These challenges often include:
- Achieving consistent long-term revenue growth
- Winning strategically critical contracts
- Improving business development performance

To help your firm meet these challenges and overcome associated

CV - ClientView LLC

obstacles, we provide highly specialized services designed specifically for government contractors who are seeking to win more Government bids, including:

Management Consulting for Growth Leadership – *from Strategy to Leadership*: Establishing strategies for revenue growth, leadership communications, business development management, strategic business planning, organizational alignment and communications strategies.

Implementing Strategy for Revenue Growth – *from Marketing to Winning Proposals*: Executing marketing, prospecting, market research, positioning, capture planning, pricing strategies proposal management and proposal writing

Revenue Growth Training – *from Training to Performance*: Developing an understanding of what your client sees as value, effective marketing to government organizations, sales calls and capture plans, win strategies and writing proposals to win.

http://www.clientviewconsulting.com

16 Acquisition Process Scenarios

Understanding the government process for acquisition has tremendous benefits for contractors, such as:

- Knowing when it is most avantageous to make a pre-RFP sales call
- Knowing the nature of information that will be of most interest for your prospect
- Improving your ability to estimate the timing of a RFP release
- Knowing what is required by the government for each step in the acquisition process
- Knowing the specific FAR requirements being address in each step in the acquisition process

RFP - Request for Proposal

There are sixteen basic approaches that the government may use under the FAR to acquire products and/or services. The scenarios are guidance documents and allow creative deviations to address the needs of specific agencies and situations. However, deviations are most likely to be variations on one of these 16 processes. Therefore, it is useful for government contractors to become familiar with the scenarios and how they are applied by the agencies within your firm's target markets.

The scenarios list all of the tasks, in their generally required sequence, that must be performed during an acquisition and their links to each specific FAR parts and subparts and to the various offices involved in each task. It is not unusual for the tasks that must be completed before an RFP can be released to require two years or more. Knowledge and familiarity with the acquisition process enables a contractor to anticipate the types of information that program managers and contract officers will find most interesting before a RFP is released.

The list below presents information for finding and downloading all of the scenarios. And following that, as an example, is a copy of the twelve page download of Acquisition Process Scenario:1. To review other Scenarios, go to their websites and download a copy.

Acquisition Process Scenario: 1
www.acquisition.gov/1_openmktnotsimplified.doc
File Format: Microsoft Word - Quick View
Acquisition Process Scenario: 1. Open Market -Not Simplified Acquisition.

APS 1

Acquisition Process Scenario: 2
https://www.acquisition.gov/2_twostepsealedbid.doc
File Format: Microsoft Word - Quick View
Acquisition Process Scenario: 2. Two Step Sealed Bid.

APS 2

Acquisition Process Scenario: 3
www.acquisition.gov/3_solesource.doc
File Format: Microsoft Word - Quick View
Acquisition Process Scenario: 3. Sole Source (Open Market –Not Simplified).

APS 3

Acquisition Process Scenario: 4
https://www.acquisition.gov/4_unsolicitedproposal.doc
File Format: Microsoft Word - Quick View
Acquisition Process Scenario: 4. Unsolicited Proposal.

APS 4

Acquisition Process Scenario: 5
https://www.acquisition.gov/5_sealedbid.doc
File Format: Microsoft Word - Quick View
Acquisition Process Scenario: 5. Sealed Bid.

APS 5

Acquisition Process Scenario: 6
https://www.acquisition.gov/6_openmktsimplified_100k-5mcom.doc
File Format: Microsoft Word - Quick View
Acquisition Process Scenario: 6. Open Market Simplified Acquisition $100,000 - 5M Commercial.

APS 6

Acquisition Process Scenario: 7
https://www.acquisition.gov/7_openmktsimplified_25-100k.doc
File Format: Microsoft Word - Quick View
Acquisition Process Scenario: 7. Open Market Simplified Acquisition $25,001 - 100,000.

APS 7

Acquisition Process Scenario: 8
https://www.acquisition.gov/8_openmktsimplified_10-25k.doc
File Format: Microsoft Word - Quick View

APS 8

Acquisition Process Scenario: 8. Open Market Simplified Acquisition $10,001 - 25,000.

APS 9

Acquisition Process Scenario: 9
https://www.acquisition.gov/9_openmktsimplified_2.5-10k.doc
File Format: Microsoft Word - Quick View
Acquisition Process Scenario: 9. Open Market Simplified Acquisition $2,501 - 10,000.

APS 10

Acquisition Process Scenario: 10
www.acquisition.gov/10_sbir.doc
File Format: Microsoft Word - Quick View
Acquisition Process Scenario: 10. Small Business Innovation Research (SBIR).

APS 11

Acquisition Process Scenario: 11
https://www.acquisition.gov/11_deliverytaskidiq.doc
File Format: Microsoft Word - Quick View
Acquisition Process Scenario: 11. Delivery / Task Orders Against Indefinite Delivery Vehicle (IDIQ).

APS 12

Acquisition Process Scenario: 12
www.acquisition.gov/12_ordersagainstfssschedule.doc
File Format: Microsoft Word - Quick View
Acquisition Process Scenario: 12. Orders Against FSS Schedule.

APS 13

Acquisition Process Scenario: 13
https://www.acquisition.gov/13_ordersagainstfssmulaward.doc
File Format: Microsoft Word - Quick View
Acquisition Process Scenario: 13. Orders Against FSS Multiple Award Schedule.

APS 14

Acquisition Process Scenario: 14
www.acquisition.gov/14_economyactorders.doc
File Format: Microsoft Word - Quick View
Acquisition Process Scenario: 14. Economy Act Orders.

APS 15

Acquisition Process Scenario: 15
https://www.acquisition.gov/15_micropurchase.doc
File Format: Microsoft Word - Quick View
Acquisition Process Scenario: 15. Micro Purchase (Stand Alone Single Purchase).

APS 16

Acquisition Process Scenario: 16
https://www.acquisition.gov/16_purchasecard.doc
File Format: Microsoft Word - Quick View
Acquisition Process Scenario: 16. Purchase Cards / Convenience Checks / Third Party Drafts (under applicable micro purchase threshold).

The next twelve pages are copied from the website cited for APS 1 and present one excellent example of the format and content of each of the 16 Scenarios. FIRM found it very helpful to identify the Acquisition Process the government was using for each of the opportunities which FIRM persued. This knowledge significantly improved the effectiveness of their efforts to improve their market position in competitive procurements and their win rate.

Figure 6.1 Example of an Acquisition Process Scenario - Next 12 pages

Acquisition Process Scenario Example

Acquisition Process Scenario: 1. Open Market -Not Simplified Acquisition

Roles: PO, BO, FO, OSDBU, AT, SSA, Offerors, PO/BO

PO	Program Office (Role performs: program management, sustainment/logistics, data, facility support, programmatics, end user)
FO	Finance Office (Role performs: accounting functions, budget functions)
AT	Acquisition Team (Role performs: Defined by FAR 1.102-3)
Offerors	Quoters, Bidders, or Offerors

Systems: C = Current, F= Future, P = Partial

BO	Buying Office (Role performs: contracting/purchasing functions)
OSDBU	Small Business
SSA	Source Selection Authority- Determines Awardee
PO/BO	Either or PO/BO

#	Activity	Description	Role	Systems C / Name	F	Information Exchanges	Control / Business Rules
1.	**Define Requirements**						
1.1	Determine Need	Draft requirement, establish budget, and seek budget approval.	PO				FAR 7.105(a), 7.107, 10.001(a) 11.002, 11.401,
1.1.1	Record Funding	Record funding.	FO				
1.1.2	Combine Requirements	Explore ability to combine requirements, explore best business arrangements (contract partnering).	BO				
1.2	Validate Funding	Validate funding line. This may include commitment or obligation depending on agency specific business procedures.	BO				OMB Circular A-11; DoD FMR Vol 2A, Chapter 2A Sec 0102; FAR 32.702
1.2.1	Validate Funding	Validate funding line and budget restrictions.	PO				
1.2.2	Validate Funding	Validate funding line and budget restrictions.	FO				
1.3	Acquisition Planning	Develop acquisition plan data.	PO				FAR: 1.102-3, 7.103, 7.105; 7.4, 14.201(a), 15.100, 15.101, 15.201(c) FAR 19.202 11.401
1.3.1	Acquisition Planning	Develop and Coordinate Acquisition Planning (Forecast and Acquisition Plan).	BO				FAR: 1.102-3, 7.103; 7.105; 7.4, 14.201(a), 15.100, 15.101, 15.201(c), 19.202
1.3.2	Validate Goals	Validate and publish goals and agency forecast. Generally done once a year.	OSDBU	X / Acqnet		• Publish goals and forecast	
				FBO	X	• Publish goals and forecast	
1.4	Purchase Request	Submit to Buying Office. Should include Statement of work/ specifications, or other requirements and evaluation criteria.	PO				15, Sec 150202; FAR 32.7
1.4.1	Communicate Purchase Request to BO	Transfer of purchase request data from PO thru FO to BO.					Agency-specific
1.5	Assigned Buyer / Contract Specialist	Buying Office analyzes requirement; assigns to buyer / contract specialist.	BO				Agency policy; FAR 7.102(b) OMB Cir A-11
2.	**Market Research**						
2.1	Follow Order of	For supplies: internal first, warehouses,	BO				FAR 8.001

Acquisition Process Scenario: 1. Open Market -Not Simplified Acquisition

Roles: PO, BO, FO, OSDBU, AT, SSA, Offerors, PO/BO

PO	Program Office (Role performs: program management, sustainment/logistics, data, facility support, programmatics, end user)
FO	Finance Office (Role performs: accounting functions, budget functions)
AT	Acquisition Team (Role performs: Defined by FAR 1.102-3)
Offerors	Quoters, Bidders, or Offerors

Systems: C = Current, F= Future, P = Partial

BO	Buying Office (Role performs: contracting/purchasing functions)
OSDBU	Small Business
SSA	Source Selection Authority- Determines Awardee
PO/BO	Either or PO/ BO

#	Activity	Description	Role	C	Name	F	Information Exchanges	Control / Business Rules
	Required Sources	UNICOR, JWOD, schedules, and open market. / For services: JWOD, UNICOR, schedules, and open market.						
2.1.1	Check Agency Excess Property	Check Agency excess property.	PO					FAR 8.001
2.1.2	Check Federal Excess Property	Check Federal excess property.	PO	X	FEDS	X	• Check Federal excess personal property	FAR 8.001
2.1.3	Check Required Sources	Check required sources i.e., JWOD & UNICOR sources.	BO	X	JWOD Website	X	• Check required source	FAR 8.7, 8.6 / 41 USC 46-48c; 18 USC 4121-4128
				X	UNICOR Website	X	• Check required source	
2.1.4	Check Federal Supply Schedules/ Multiple Award Contracts / GWACs	Check Federal Supply Schedules/ Multiple Award Contracts / GWAC.	PO/ BO	X	eCatalog	X	• Check Supply Schedules • Check GWACs	FAR 8.4; 16.505; 41 USC 102-36.65
				X	Advantage	X	• Check Supply Schedules	
				X	Buyers.gov	X	• Reverse auction for IT against FSS and FTS contracts	
				X	FBO	X	• Check for potential combining of requirements	
2.2	Conduct Market Survey	Determine industrial category (NAICS) and size standards. Gather market survey findings.	BO	X	Census Website	X	• Check for specific NAICS	FAR 6.102; 19.201; FAR 19.303
				X	CCR/BPN	X	• Use NAICS to find potential Offerors	
2.2.1	Validate Market Survey Findings	Validate NAICS. Validate small business opportunities.	OSDBU	X	Census Website	X	• Check with a specific NAICS	FAR 6.102, 19.201, 19.303
				X	CCR/BPN	X	• Use NAICS to find potential Offerors	
2.3	Issue Sources Sought Notice	Posting in newspapers, single point of government entry, trade magazines, other specialized web sites.	BO	X	FBO	X	• Post synopsis for sources sought	FAR 5.002, 5.101; 15 USC 637(e), 41 USC 416

Acquisition Process Scenario: 1. Open Market -Not Simplified Acquisition

Roles: PO, BO, FO, OSDBU, AT, SSA, Offerors, PO/BO

Role		**Systems:** C = Current, F= Future, P = Partial
PO	Program Office (Role performs: program management, sustainment/logistics, data, facility support, programmatics, end user)	
	BO	Buying Office (Role performs: contracting/purchasing functions)
FO	Finance Office (Role performs: accounting functions, budget functions)	
	OSDBU	Small Business
AT	Acquisition Team (Role performs: Defined by FAR 1.102-3)	
	SSA	Source Selection Authority- Determines Awardee
Offerors	Quoters, Bidders, or Offerors	
	PO/BO	Either or PO/BO

#	Activity	Description	Role	Systems C	Systems Name	Systems F	Information Exchanges	Control / Business Rules
2.3.1	Establish Information Library	Drawings, specifications and other related documents. (Role may shift to PO)	BO	X	FBO	x	• Upload documents	FAR 15.201(f); 11.201; 5.102(b)(iii) 14.211(a)
					FedTeds	X	• Upload documents	
2.3.2	Assess Responses From Sources Sought	Receive responses and coordinate evaluations by the Acquisition Team.	BO	X	CCR/BPN	X	• Compare NAICS • Assess capabilities – Validate interest in type of requirement	FAR 15.202 14.101(a), (b)
				X	ProNET		• Assess capabilities – Validate business size	
				X	FPDS	X	• Assess capabilities – validate experience	
					PPIRS	X	• Assess capabilities – validate past performance	
2.4	Negotiate Set-aside	Prepare a position/recommendation document.	BO					FAR 19.5
2.4.1	Review Recommendations	Review and resolve position/recommendation.	OSDBU					
3.0	**Issue Synopsis/RFQ/ RFP / Invitation for Bid (IFB)**	Issue pre-solicitation synopsis advertising that requirements need to be filled.						
3.1	Post Notice of Contract Action (Pre-solicitation Synopsis)	Post to Federal Single Point of Entry, newspapers, periodicals, trade journals, and professional journals.	BO	X	FBO	X	• Advertising requirement	FAR 5.201(a)

Acquisition Process Scenario: 1. Open Market -Not Simplified Acquisition

Roles: PO, BO, FO, OSDBU, AT, SSA, Offerors, PO/BO **Systems:** C= Current, F= Future, P = Partial

PO	Program Office (Role performs: program management, sustainment/logistics, data, facility support, programmatics, end user)
BO	Buying Office (Role performs: contracting/purchasing functions)
FO	Finance Office (Role performs: accounting functions, budget functions)
OSDBU	Small Business
AT	Acquisition Team (Role performs: Defined by FAR 1.102-3)
SSA	Source Selection Authority- Determines Awardee
Offerors	Quoters, Bidders, or Offerors
PO/BO	Either or PO/ BO

#	Activity	Description	Role	C	Systems Name	F	Information Exchanges	Control / Business Rules
3.1.1	Post combined synopsis/solicitation	Post combined synopsis/solicitation.	BO	X	FBO		• Advertising requirement & post solicitation	FAR 12.603
3.1.2	Process IVL	Enabling Interested Vendors List (IVL). (Optional)	BO	X	FBO	X	• Enable Interested Vendors List per solicitation	FAR 14.205, 13.104, 13.102
					BPN	X	• Use NAICS to develop potential consideration list	
3.2	Modify Synopsis	Modify Synopsis.	BO	X	FBO		• Modify synopsis	FAR 5.201(a)
3.2.1	Amend Combined synopsis-Solicitation	Amend combined synopsis-solicitation.	BO	X	FBO		• Amend combined synopsis-solicitation	FAR: 12.102 (b), 13.105, 14.208, 15.206,
3.3	Pre-Solicitation Process	Pre-Solicitation Process.						
3.3.1	Develop Selection Plan	Section L: Instructions to Offerors. Section M: Evaluation Criteria (Price, Quality, Past Performance); Establishing evaluation factors and significant sub-factors, e.g. that would fall in to source selection plan. Coordinate with PO, FO, OSDBU, and Legal.	BO					FAR: 12.203, 12.303, 13.106-1(a) (2), 13.106-2, 13.106-2(b), 13.106-3 (a), 14.201-5 (b) – (c), 14.201-8, 14.206-6, 15.1, 15.304, 15.305 10 USC 2305, 41 USC 253a
3.3.2	Build Solicitation	Develops and coordinates review of formal solicitation. This includes technical requirements provided and reviewed by the PO. The method of procurement (RFP, IFB, and RFQ) is determined and the Legal Office reviews for legal sufficiency.	BO	X	DOL – Wage Determination (Davis-Bacon)	X	• Extract wage determination (post in the solicitation for construction)	FAR 15.203-204, 14.201, 12.303, FAR 12.04, 13.106-1, 2.101
				X	NTIS / SCA Wage Determination	X	• Obtain service contract wage determinations	
3.4	Solicitation							

79

Acquisition Process Scenario: 1. Open Market -Not Simplified Acquisition

Roles: PO, BO, FO, OSDBU, AT, SSA, Offerors, PO/BO
Systems: C = Current, F= Future, P = Partial

PO	Program Office (Role performs: program management, sustainment/logistics, data, facility support, programmatics, end user)
FO	Finance Office (Role performs: accounting functions, budget functions)
AT	Acquisition Team (Role performs: Defined by FAR 1.102-3)
Offerors	Quoters, Bidders, or Offerors
BO	Buying Office (Role performs: contracting/purchasing functions)
OSDBU	Small Business
SSA	Source Selection Authority- Determines Awardee
PO/BO	Either or PO/BO

#	Activity	Description	Role	Systems C	Systems Name	Systems F	Information Exchanges	Control / Business Rules
	Process							
3.4.1	Pre-Solicitation Contact with Potential Offerors	Pre solicitation conferences, one-on-ones, draft solicitations, and other reviews by potential Offerors to obtain feedback and publicize.	BO	X	FBO	x	• Push page updates to IVs	FAR 12.102 (b), 15.201, 13.104, 14.207, 14.211
3.4.2	Issue Solicitation	Issue solicitation.	BO	X	FBO	X	• Issue / post solicitation	FAR 5.003, 5.102(a), 12.102 (b), 13.106-1, 14.203, 15.205,
					FedTEDS	X	• Upload technical drawings	
3.4.3	Solicitation Inquiries	Post solicitation Inquiries (Vendor questions, concerns, and clarifications) obtained either by written communication or from a pre-proposal conference go through Contracting Office.	BO	X	FBO	X	• Post responses to inquiries	FAR 12.102 (b), 13.106-1, 14.203, 15.206, 15.201(f); 15.303(c)
3.4.4	Amend Solicitation	Amend solicitation.	BO	X	FBO	X	• Post amendments to solicitations	FAR 12.102 (b), 12.603 (b) (4), 13.105 (a), 14.208, 15.206
3.4.5	Respond to Solicitation Protest	Can happen at any time before receipt of proposals. Solicitation protests can go to: GAO, Federal Court, Contracting Officer.	BO					FAR 12.102 b, 13.106-3(c), 14.408-8, 15.507, 33.1
4.	Evaluate Responses	Evaluate Responses activities based on RFP						
4.1	Receive Response	Receive response.	BO			X	• Receive electronic vendor responses (use this wording for invoices)	FAR 15.207-208
4.2	Conduct Initial Evaluation	Determine responsiveness.	BO	X	CCR		• Check for existence of registration	FAR 15.304-305
					BPN	X	• Validate vendor information Check far Reference for order	

Acquisition Process Scenario: 1. Open Market -Not Simplified Acquisition

Roles: PO, BO, FO, OSDBU, AT, SSA, PO/BO

PO	Program Office (Role performs: program management, sustainment/logistics, data, facility support, programmatics, end user)
BO	Buying Office (Role performs: contracting/purchasing functions)
FO	Finance Office (Role performs: accounting functions, budget functions)
OSDBU	Small Business
AT	Acquisition Team (Role performs: Defined by FAR 1.102-3)
SSA	Source Selection Authority- Determines Awardee
Offerors	Quoters, Bidders, or Offerors
PO/BO	Either or PO/ BO

Systems: C = Current, F = Future, P = Partial

#	Activity	Description	Role	Systems C	Systems Name	Systems F	Information Exchanges	Control / Business Rules
4.3	Evaluate Business Proposal	Buying Office requests evaluators; transmit documents to evaluators, evaluates price/costs, terms and conditions.	BO		ORCA	X	• Retrieve representations and certifications (R&C)	FAR 15.3, 15.303(a)(4), 15.305(a), 15.305(a)(3)
4.4	Evaluate Technical Proposal	Evaluate technical proposal.	PO					FAR 13.305(a)(1), 15.3, 15.303(a)(4), 15.305(a), 15.305(a)(3)
4.4.1	Evaluate Past Performance	Review both past and current performance utilizing online tools and telephone surveys of references	BO	X	PPIRS	x	• Check past performance information	FAR 15.305(a)(2)
4.5	Request Clarifications	Clarifications plus exchanges before establishment of competitive range, to determine relative ranking of Offerors absent discussion.	BO					FAR 15.306(a) and (b)
4.6	Determine Competitive Range	Narrow vender pool to those vendors that have a reasonable chance to receive an award. Range is determined based on outcome of evaluation.	BO					FAR 15.306(c): 10 USC 2305(b)(4), 41 USC 253b(d)
4.6.1	Notify Exclusions and Perform Pre-Award Debriefing	Notify vendors outside the competitive range and perform pre-award debriefing if requested.	BO					FAR 15.306(c)(3) & (4), 15.505 (only for negotiated)
4.7	Address Pre-Award Protests	Protests can go to GAO, Fed Court, or Contracting Officer and may occur any time before award.	BO					FAR 12.102 (b), 13.106-3 (c), 14.408-8, 15.507, 33.1
4.8	Exchanges with Offerors	At request of the contracting officer. Can include: requirements, resources, cost/price, schedule, place of delivery / performance, technical approach, and provide an opportunity to correct deficiencies and make clarifications.	BO	X	DOL Wage Determination Web Site (Davis-Bacon)	X	• Extract wage determination from Dept of Labor and post in the solicitation for construction	FAR 15.306(d)
				X	NTIS / SCA Wage Determination	X	• Obtain service contract wage determinations	
4.8.1	Receipt of Proposal	Receive proposal revisions including final offer as a result of ongoing exchange with Offeror.	BO					FAR 15.306, 15.307

Acquisition Process Scenario: 1. Open Market -Not Simplified Acquisition

Roles: PO, BO, FO, OSDBU, AT, SSA, Offerors, PO/BO

PO	Program Office (Role performs: program management, sustainment/logistics, data, facility support, programmatics, end user)
FO	Finance Office (Role performs: accounting functions, budget functions)
AT	Acquisition Team (Role performs: Defined by FAR 1.102-3)
Offerors	Quoters, Bidders, or Offerors

Systems: C = Current, F= Future, P = Partial

BO	Buying Office (Role performs: contracting/purchasing functions)
OSDBU	Small Business
SSA	Source Selection Authority- Determines Awardee
PO/BO	Either or PO/BO

#	Activity	Description	Role	Systems C	Systems Name	Systems F	Information Exchanges	Control / Business Rules
	Revisions							
4.8.2	Evaluation of Proposal Revisions		BO					FAR 15.305
4.8.2.1	Evaluate Revised Business Proposal	Transmit revised documents to evaluators; Evaluate price/costs, and terms and conditions.	BO					FAR 13.305(a)(1), 15.3
4.8.2.2	Evaluate Revised Technical Proposal	Evaluate revised technical proposal.	PO					FAR 13.305(a)(1), 15.3,
4.8.3	Conclusion of Exchanges	Common cut off date for final proposal revision.	BO					FAR 15.307(b)
4.8.4	Receipt of Final Proposal Revisions	Receive final proposal revisions as a result of conclusion of exchanges.	BO					FAR 15.307(b)
4.9	Pre-Award Surveys and Approvals	Verify eligibility of prospective awardee thru EEO clearance (as applicable), DCAA & DCMA	BO	X	DOL pre-award Website,	x	• Check vendor EEO	FAR 9.1; 9.4; 22.805(a)
				X	EPLS	X	• Obtain EPLS status	
					BPN	X	• Obtain EPLS status	
					D&B	X	• Check financials	
4.10	Source Selection Decision	Includes responsibility determination, cost technical trade offs, justification of selection, and debarred list.	SSA					FAR 15.308
5.0	**Issue Award**							
5.1	Verify Funds Availability	Ensure sufficient funds are available for proposed award value. This may include obligation depending on agency specific business procedures.	BO					FAR 32.702
5.2	Prepare Award	Assemble and prepare award documentation. Execute procurement instrument.	BO					FAR 14.408-1, 15.204, 15.504

Acquisition Process Scenario: 1. Open Market -Not Simplified Acquisition

Roles: PO, BO, FO, OSDBU, AT, SSA, Offerors, PO/BO

Role	Description
PO	Program Office (Role performs: program management, sustainment/logistics, data, facility support, programmatics, end user)
FO	Finance Office (Role performs: accounting functions, budget functions)
AT	Acquisition Team (Role performs: Defined by FAR 1.102-3)
Offerors	Quoters, Bidders, or Offerors

Systems: C = Current, F= Future, P = Partial

Role	Description
BO	Buying Office (Role performs: contracting/purchasing functions)
OSDBU	Small Business
SSA	Source Selection Authority- Determines Awardee
PO/BO	Either or PO/ BO

#	Activity	Description	Role	C	Name	F	Information Exchanges	Control / Business Rules
5.3	Prepare Management Award Information	Develop and submit federal procurement data regarding specific current award.	BO	X	FPDS	X	• Report Information	FAR 4.6
					GWAC Index	X	• Post award data	
5.4	Issue Award Notices	Post required notices: • Pre-award notices under set- asides this is an intent to award to vendor (only for vendors in competitive range) • Congress (as applicable), • Post award notice (FBO); • Unsuccessful Offerors • DOL (as applicable)	BO	X	FBO	X	• Post award notice	FAR 5.303, 12.102 (b), 13.106-3(c) 14.409-1 (b), 15.503, ; agency regs e.g. DFARS 204.6 for reports to Congress
				X	ECats	X	• Post vendor data to catalogs	
					DOL	X	• Inform Award of service based contract performance	
				X	Sub-net		• Post subcontracting opportunities	
				X	FACNET	x	• EDI Transaction • Potential for electronic transmission to Congress	
5.5	Distribute Award Document	Send document / notification to: • Finance office • Program Office • OSDBU • Contractor • Contract Administration • DCAA • Security	BO	P	EDA	X	• Post all award documents to provide for internal notifications	FAR 4.201
					CADO	X	• Post contract award documents to provide for transparency and visibility	
5.6	Perform Post Award Debriefing	One-on-one discussion with non-selected Offerors of the aspects of their proposal and top-level information of the winner only. Coordinate with Legal and Program Office	BO					FAR 14.409-1(b), 15.506
5.7	Address Post-Award Protest	Resolve post award protests, thru Alternative Dispute resolution (ADR) or court. Rule 4 file is developed. This activity is coordinated with Legal Office.	BO	X	GAO website		• Conduct legal research	FAR 12.102(b), 13.106-3 (c), 14.408-8, 15.507, 33.1
				X	Court of Claims Web site		• Conduct legal research	

Acquisition Process Scenario: 1. Open Market -Not Simplified Acquisition

Roles: PO, BO, FO, OSDBU, AT, SSA, Offerors, PO/BO

Systems: C = Current, F= Future, P = Partial

Role	Description
PO	Program Office (Role performs: program management, sustainment/logistics, data, facility support, programmatics, end user)
FO	Finance Office (Role performs: accounting functions, budget functions)
AT	Acquisition Team (Role performs: Defined by FAR 1.102-3)
Offerors	Quoters, Bidders, or Offerors
BO	Buying Office (Role performs: contracting/purchasing functions)
OSDBU	Small Business
SSA	Source Selection Authority- Determines Awardee
PO/BO	Either or PO/ BO

#	Activity	Description	Role	Systems C	Systems Name	Systems F	Information Exchanges	Control / Business Rules
				X	Lexus/Nexus & Others		• Conduct legal research	
6.	**Monitor Performance/Contract Administration**							
6.1	Conduct Post-Award Orientation	Conduct post award conferences exchanging information to verify baseline program performance, and to create consistent expectations between the contractor and government team. Activity may be worked in conjunction with PO and Administrative Contracting Officer (ACO).	BO					FAR 42.5
6.2	Issue Notice to Proceed	Provide authority to proceed with contract performance (For Construction Contracts Only).	BO					FAR 36.213(e)
6.3	Monitor & Document Performance	Communication and documentation between Government and Contractor regarding quality and timeliness. Accomplished by COTR under authority of Contracting Officer (PCO or ACO).	PO	X	DOD CPARS	x	• Post Performance Information	FAR 42, 46.4
				X	NIH CPS	x	• Post Performance Information	
				X	NASA PPDBS	x	• Post Performance Information	
				X	Army PPMIS		• Post Performance Information	
				X	FDIC		• Post Performance Information	
				X	Education		• Post Performance Information	
6.3.1	Inspect Goods and or Services	Preparation and completion of receiving documentation (e.g. DD250).	PO		PPIRS	x	• Collecting passive past performance information as it relates to	FAR 46.5

Acquisition Process Scenario: 1. Open Market -Not Simplified Acquisition

Roles: PO, BO, FO, OSDBU, AT, SSA, Offerors, PO/BO

Role	Description		Systems
PO	Program Office (Role performs: program management, sustainment/logistics, data, facility support, programmatics, end user)		C = Current, F= Future, P = Partial
		BO	Buying Office (Role performs: contracting/purchasing functions)
FO	Finance Office (Role performs: accounting functions, budget functions)	OSDBU	Small Business
AT	Acquisition Team (Role performs: Defined by FAR 1.102-3)	SSA	Source Selection Authority- Determines Awardee
Offerors	Quoters, Bidders, or Offerors	PO/BO	Either or PO/ BO

#	Activity	Description	Role	Systems C	Systems Name	Systems F	Information Exchanges	Control / Business Rules
6.3.2	Accept Goods and or Services	For each contract line item number.	BO/PO				timeliness quality, and delivery	FAR 46.5
6.3.3	Manage Property	Adjust agency property (includes government furnished items or equipment or contractor purchased items or equipment).	PO	X	FEDS or DRMO		• Identify disposal of excess contractor acquired property	
6.4	Process Contract Changes	Issue modifications or change orders. Contracting Officer working in coordination with PO, ACO, FO, & Legal.	BO					FAR 43
6.4.1	Verify Funding	Ensure sufficient funds are available for proposed award value.	BO					FAR 32.702
6.4.2	Prepare Management Award Information	Develop and submit federal procurement data regarding specific current award.	BO	X	FPDS-NG	X	• Report Management Information	FAR 4.6
					GWAC Index	X	• Post award Management data on GWAC index as applicable	
6.4.3	Issue Novation Agreements	Administrative modification to the contract due to changing contractor name, banking information, and addresses. ACO / PCO must approve name change.	BO		BPN	X	• Notification of name change	FAR 42.12
6.5	Assignment of Claims	Re-designate remittance entity.	BO	P	CCR/BPN	X	• Change payee (EFT)	FAR 32.8
7.	Approve Payment							
7.1	Receive Invoice	Must meet requirements set forth in contract. Role is dependent on how agency writes contract.	BO/ FO/ PO					FAR 52.232-25
7.2	Submit Invoice to Finance Office	Communicate approved invoice to Finance Office.	BO/ PO					FAR 32.9
7.3	Match Invoice to	Ensure goods and or services have been performed satisfactory against contract	FO					FAR 46.502 FAR 32.702

Acquisition Process Scenario: 1. Open Market -Not Simplified Acquisition

Roles: PO, BO, FO, OSDBU, AT, SSA, Offerors, PO/BO

Role	Description
PO	Program Office (Role performs: program management, sustainment/logistics, data, facility support, programmatics, end user)
FO	Finance Office (Role performs: accounting functions, budget functions)
AT	Acquisition Team (Role performs: Defined by FAR 1.102-3)
Offerors	Quoters, Bidders, or Offerors

Systems: C = Current, F= Future, P = Partial

BO	Buying Office (Role performs: contracting/purchasing functions)
OSDBU	Small Business
SSA	Source Selection Authority- Determines Awardee
PO/BO	Either or PO/ BO

#	Activity	Description	Role	Systems C	Systems Name	Systems F	Information Exchanges	Control / Business Rules
	Receiving Report and Obligating Document	requirements.						
8.	**Pay Vendor**							
8.1	Receive Approved Invoice	Finance Office receives an approved invoice thru Buying Office.	FO			x	• Submission of invoices from vendors	DoD FMR Vol 10, Chapter 9, Sec 0903
8.2	Ensure Availability of Funds	Verify accounting records (matching process).	FO					FAR 32.702
8.3	Verify EFT Information	Finance Office originally obtained EFT information when they received the obligating document. This information must be verified before payment.	FO	P	CCR/BPN	X	• Obtain EFT data	FAR 32.11
8.4	Process Payment	Produce payment requests and create an electronic voucher that is transmitted to Treasury for disbursement.	FO					FAR 32.9
8.4.1	Verify Off-sets	Verify if payment should be reduced due to amounts owed to government by contractor.	Treasury, DFAS	X	TOPs	X	• Verify payment e.g. TIN	Debt Collection Improvement Act PL 104-134
8.4.2	Transfer Funds	Pay Vendor via check or EFT.	Federal Reserve, DFAS					
9.	**Close Out**							
9.1	Certify All Work has been Completed	Check that all requirements under contract have been satisfactorily met and that there are no outstanding claims or judgments.	PO					FAR 4.804-5(a)
9.2	Settle Any Claims	Negotiate outstanding claims and obtain release of claims.	BO					FAR 4.804-5(a)(14)
9.3	Issue Final Past Performance Evaluation	Produce final performance evaluation identifying quality and timeliness throughout the history of the contract.	PO	X / x	DOD CPARS / NIH CPS	X / x	• Update performance data for close-out • Update performance data for close-out	FAR 42.15

Acquisition Process Scenario: 1. Open Market -Not Simplified Acquisition

Roles: PO, BO, FO, OSDBU, AT, SSA, Offerors, PO/BO

PO	Program Office (Role performs: program management, sustainment/logistics, data, facility support, programmatics, end user)	
FO	Finance Office (Role performs: accounting functions, budget functions)	
AT	Acquisition Team (Role performs: Defined by FAR 1.102-3)	
Offerors	Quoters, Bidders, or Offerors	

Systems: C = Current, F= Future, P = Partial

BO	Buying Office (Role performs: contracting/purchasing functions)
OSDBU	Small Business
SSA	Source Selection Authority- Determines Awardee
PO/BO	Either or PO/ BO

#	Activity	Description	Role	Systems			Information Exchanges	Control / Business Rules
				Name	C	F		
				NASA PPDBS	x	x	• Update performance data for close-out	
9.4	Pay Final Invoice	See Pay vendor 8.1-8.42						FAR 4.804-5(b), 52.222-7, 52.52.222-41(k)
9.5	Maintain Archival Contract Files	Maintain official contract records in accordance with agency procedures and NARA requirements.	BO	FPDS-NG		X	• Report close-out information (12c FPDS-NG requirement reason for modification "closed-out")	FAR 4.805
						X	• Record Mgt per NARA	

7

Starting Steps

Pre-Start Organizational Decisions

- Determine if you are a provider of services, products or both (there are varying implications for each path)
- Conduct a market survey to determine if there is sufficient government demand for your products or services
- Develop a business plan and determine how you can make a profit and over what timeframe
- Determine which type of legal entity you want to be (Corporation? Sole Proprietorship? Limited Liability Company?) and seek legal assistance setting up your business
- Determine a name for your business (Legal and DBA (if applicable))
- Obtain an EIN from IRS
- Select a state in which to Register your business for operations and file organization papers
- Obtain a DUNS number from D&B. Call D&B at 866-705-5711 or via e-mail to govt@dnb.com if you do not have a DUNS number.

   http://www.whitehouse.gov/sites/default/files/omb/ grants/duns_num_guide.pdf

   http://www.sba.gov/content/getting-d-u-n-s- number

   http://www.dnb.com

- Identify the NAICS Codes for your products and services. "Take advantage of our free online NAICS and SIC Code Search Tools to determine your Company's NAICS and SIC Code - Search by Keyword or Drill Down by Industry. Click here to view the SBA's Small Business Size Standards."

   http://www.naics.com

- Register your business with the Fed Gov't (and then receive a government provided CAGE code). "The System for Award Management (SAM) is a free web site that consolidates the capabilities you used to find in CCR/FedReg, ORCA, and EPLS. Future phases of SAM will add the capabilities of other systems used in Federal procurement and awards processes. The System for Award Management (SAM) is combining federal

procurement systems and the Catalog of Federal Domestic Assistance into one new system. This consolidation is being done in phases. The first phase of SAM includes the functionality from the following systems:
* Central Contractor Registry (CCR)
* Federal Agency Registration (Fedreg)
* Online Representations and Certifications Application
* Excluded Parties List System (EPLS)"

https://www.sam.gov/portal/public/SAM/

Contracting Issues and Decisions

- Learn about how the government operates and buys from its markets
- Understand basic government contracting laws and regulations
- Seek help from professionals

Operational Decisions

- Payroll, Insurance (liability, building, etc.), Infrastructure, , website, buy or lease a facility, email, phones, computers systems and printers
- Understand and address Legal issues related to your employees, workplace, services (e.g. liability) and/or products (e.g. environmental; liability)

Marketing Decisions

- Memberships in advocacy groups (e.g. NDIA)
- Website
- Marketing Collateral
- Advertising
- Conferences
- Get leads. There are free sources of information about planned Government acquisitions that may be opp[ortunities for your company. Federal Business Opportuinities is the most comprehensive source but is difficult to use for broad market surveys. However, it is terrific for researching specific single opportunities. You enter your search criteria and it will find new opportunities that fit your requirements.

https://www.fbo.gov

Financial Decisions

- Retaining the CPA for your business
- Operating Cash Flow, Bank Accounts, Chart of Accounts, Accounting and Book keeping

8

End Notes

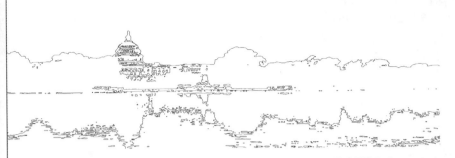

[1] "More than 600,000 firms registered in the CCR" information provided by Federal Contractor Registry (*FCR) by email on December 3, 2012.
**"There are over 600,000 business entities that are currently active in the CCR. Thank you for contacting us.
FCR Customer Service"**

FCR

[2] Defense Contract Audit Agency - 2011 Year in Review
"In 2011, DCAA examined over $125B in defense contractor costs and issued over 7,000 audit reports. These reports recommended $11.9B in cost reductions. Overall, DCAA's efforts resulted in $3.5B in net savings to the Government. Based on these net savings, the return on taxpayers' investment in DCAA was approximately $5.80 for each dollar invested. This $5.80 return represents actual savings that DoD can reinvest in other ways to help the warfighter."

DCAA

[3] Gary A. Dunbar's career spans from 1966 to 2012 with his initial experience in U. S. Government Contracts in the early 1970s. His professional experience was totally in the private sector with various technology firms and included positions from Draftsman to Chief Executive Officer and membership on six Boards of Directors.

Gary A Dunbar

Career highlights include:

Significant Client Achievements

- Over $6.5 billion in new contract wins including
- $2.35 billion Department of Defense contract
- $1.6 billion Department of Energy contract
- $61 million Terrorist Screening Center contract
- Client's revenue grows 40% per year
- Client's contract portfolio value grew from $0 to over $1B in four years
- Client's annual revenue tripled in four years
- Client launched a five-year growth plan increasing revenue more than five fold
- Client's competitive contract "WIN RATE" improved from 20% to over 50% in two years

Government Clients (Business development experience)

- Department of Defense

- Department of Energy
- Department of Interior
- Environmental Protection Agency
- Defense Threat Reduction Agency
- Terrorist Screening Center
- Agency for International Development
- United Nations
- Government of Ukraine
- City of New York
- World Bank
- National Counterterrorism Center
- Defense Intelligence Agency
- U. S. Army Tank-Automotive Command

Career Positions

- Senior Vice President and General Manager of a management, technology, and environmental consulting subsidiary.
- Executive Vice President and Chief Operating Officer of a nuclear engineering and environmental technology company.
- Founding President and Chief Executive Officer of an environmental consulting company.
- Founder and President of a business development consulting company

Value Delivery Strategy	[4] "The Discipline of Market Leaders" by Michael Treacy and Fred Wiersema, Perseus Books, Cambridge, Massachusetts 1995
Solution Selling	[5] "Solution Selling" by Michael T. Bosworth, McGraw-Hill, 1995
Shared Vision or Big Picture	[6] "The Fifth Discipline Fieldbook" by Peter Senge, Art Kleiner, Charlotte Robert, Richard B. Ross, and Bryan J. Smith, Doubleday, New York, New York 1994

Tools, Templates and Guidelines

FIRM's business development tools, templates and guidelines were provided by CleintView and are listed below. Many of these have been presented in the preceeding pages and the other listed items serve as a tickler file of ideas and suggestions for improving your career or your firm's business development. The items are arranged in groups matching the time phases in FIRM's business development framework.

Items reviewed in this book are in bold font.

Revenue Growth Strategy

- **REVENUE GROWTH/BUSINESS DEVELOPMENT FRAMEWORK**
- **BD RESPONSIBILITY MATRIX**
- ROAD MAP PLANNING
- PLANNING GUIDANCE AND TEMPLATES
     STRATEGIC PLAN
     BUSINESS PLAN
     MARKETING PLAN
     SALES PLAN
- ROBUST VISION /AMBITION WORKBOOK
- STRATEGY WORKSHOP FACILITATION – TEAM ALIGNMENT
- TECHNOLOGY MARKET ASSESSMENT
- REVENUE ANALYSIS METHOD
- STRATEGIC PLAN GUIDE
- SAC GUIDANCE
- 100 DAY STRATEGIC PLAN
- **BUSINESS PLAN GUIDE**
- MARKETING PLAN GUIDE
- SALES PLAN GUIDE
- CONSULTANT DIRECTORY
- **BD METRIC BASED POSITIONS DESCRIPTIONS**
- **COMPENSATION AND INCENTIVE PLANNING**
- BUSINESS DEVELOPMENT TRAINING
     STRATEGY ANALYSIS AND PLANNING
     MARKET ENTRY - DIVERSIFICATION
     BUSINESS DEVELOPMENT MANAGEMENT

Marketing

- **VALUE DELIVERY ANALYSIS**
- NICHE ANALYSIS

- MARKET SURVEY
- COMPELLING MESSAGE DEVELOPMENT
- PERSUASION TOOLS
- NEEDS ANALYSIS GUIDANCE AND TEMPLATES
- CUSTOMER DATABASE
- KEY CLIENT MANAGEMENT PROGRAM GUIDANCE
- CLIENT COMMUNICATION PROGRAM GUIDANCE
- TRADE SHOW KEEPERS - USEFUL AND VALUABLE INFORMATION CREATION
- SALES PLAN GUIDE
- DEFINING MARKETING NEEDS FOR SALES PLANS
- DIRECTORY FORMATS
    - CONSULTANT DIRECTORY
    - COMPETITOR DIRECTORY
    - CLIENT DIRECTORY
- TRAINING - VALUE DELIVERY STRATEGY

Prospecting

- **LEAD INVESTMENT ASSESSMENT**
- OPPORTUNITY QUALIFICATION FORM
- **BUSINESS DEVELOPMENT TRACKING AND MANAGEMENT GUIDANCE**
- **16 ACQUISITION MODELS**
- **OPPORTUNITY ENTRY INTO TRACKING SYSTEM**
- **OPPORTUNITY REVENUE FORECASTING**
- **OPPORTUNITY TRACKING & REPORTING**
- QUARTERLY SALES REPORTS AND ASSESSMENT
- DATABASE PROSPECTING TECHNIQUES
- NETWORK PROSPECTING TECHNIQUES

Positioning

- **OPPORTUNITY INVESTMENT ASSESSMENT**
- CAPTURE PLAN APPROVAL FORM
- **CAPTURE PLAN GUIDANCE AND TEMPLATE**
- SALES CALL GUIDANCE
- WHITE PAPER GUIDANCE
- DISCRIMINATOR WORKSHEET
- COMPETITOR ANALYSIS GUIDANCE AND TEMPLATE
- TEAMING GUIDANCE AND TEMPLATE
- QUARTERLY TARGET COMPARISON WITH STRATEGIC OBJECTIVES
- TARGET REVENUE FORECASTING
- POSITIONING IMPLEMENTATION TRACKING & REPORTING
- DATABASES AND NETWORKS
- TRAINING
    - SALES CALLS
    - PROCUREMENT FOCUS
    - CAPTURE PLAN
- POSITIONING DELIVERABLES LIST

- **TARGET INVESTMENT ASSESSMENT**
- **PROPOSAL APPROVAL FORM**
- PROPOSAL CREATION AND PRODUCTION MANAGEMENT GUIDANCE AND TEMPLATE
- CONTRACT RISK AND MITIGATION ASSESSMENT GUIDANCE AND TEMPLATE
- PROPOSAL SECTION GUIDES
- PROPOSAL REVIEW GUIDES – GOLD, PINK, RED, & GREEN
- QUARTERLY PROPOSAL COMPARISON WITH STRATEGIC OBJECTIVES
- PIP REVENUE FORECASTING

- TRAINING
    - FUNDAMENTALS
    - BEST VALUE
    - OUTLINE TO WIN
- ARTICULATING STRATEGY
- PROPOSAL TECHNIQUES
- PROPOSAL MANAGEMENT

- CONTRACT PERFORMANCE ASSESSMENT GUIDANCE AND TEMPLATE
- QUALITY ASSURANCE GUIDANCE AND TEMPLATE
- COST AND SCHEDULE STATUS REPORTING GUIDANCE AND TEMPLATE
- INTEGRATED MASTER PLAN AND INTEGRATED MASTER SCHEDULE
- PROJECT SCHEDULE GUIDANCE AND TEMPLATE
- REQUIREMENT TRACEABILITY GUIDANCE AND TEMPLATE
- CONTRACT REFERENCE ARCHIVE
- **ANNUAL OPERATIONS PLANNED AND ACTUAL PERFORMANCE MONITORING**